CORDEE
3a De Montfort Street, Leicester LE1 7HD

Published by Cordee 1989

Copyright © Heather MacDermid 1989
Maps Cordee

British Library Cataloguing in Publication Data
MacDermid, Heather
   Circular walks between Foxton Locks and Rutland Water.
   1. Leicester.   East Leicestershire.   Visitors' guides
   I. Title
   914.25'4

ISBN 1–871890–05–5

Acknow

I should lik

to Stan Jam   n
the walkir   e
instruction: o
researching   e
have walke

to Mr and Mrs Clements of Tilton for their knowledge of the walks in their area and the care and attention to detail they have given to the instructions:

to all those friends who have walked with me to produce this book and to make the task so pleasurable:

to past and present members of Leicestershire Footpath Association for their knowledge of the countryside, for their love of these pathways and for their good company.

Illustrations	Jean Harrison
Design and Maps	E. Holmes
Cover Design	Ivan Cumberpatch

A

Preface

This Book is a companion volume to Walks around Charnwood but the area is very different. We leave the granite walls and buildings and the rugged volcanic rocks of Charnwood and find instead East Leicestershire's rolling hills and valleys with their lovely Collyweston-tiled ironstone and limestone villages.

The Landscape is more varied, less unified than Charnwood and it hasn't proved possible to give one long walk to take you round the whole area. I have, however been able to offer a greater variety of distances for you to walk and a lot more lovely little villages for you to see nestling in farming country, separated by little hills and small patches of woodland or fox coverts.

The Introductions to each Walk indicate items of interest, places to stop, to start, to join the walk or to leave it to extend or to shorten it.

The Notes to Places of Interest are meant to be read either before or after your walk or while you wander round the site or when you sit down to rest! I have presumed that on short walks you might be interested in knowing a little about the places you visit, but I have separated them from the walking instructions so they are an optional extra.

The Walks are all circular, so that those who come by car can return to their starting point. These starting points are often off the beaten track and I have not attempted to provide details of public transport. But these can be obtained from the Busline telephone enquiry service on Leics. 313391 and I have no doubt that some dedicated walkers with inside knowledge of the intricacies of bus time tables will manage to travel by public transport and complete all the walks.

Figures of Eight You have here a series of short walks connecting little villages or hamlets which are usually no more than two miles apart. The walks can be extended by joining them together or by inserting one into the other. They take the form of figures of eight or clover leaves, and enable you to explore an area in different directions on different days if you wish. I hope that by following the instructions carefully you will be able to master the art of composing a walk of the length you really like.

Stepping Stones Each section acts like a stepping stone to take you out and around this south eastern corner of Leicestershire and into Rutland. Many of these sections are centred on places which provide refreshment and shelter!

Instructions for Walking have deliberately been kept free of description and explanation because the aim is to keep you on the right path with a minimum of distraction.

Special Items of Interest and particularly good views have, however, been briefly indicated, so that you do not miss a good opportunity to see them when the moment arrives: these are indented to highlight them and separate them from the instructions.

In adjoining Circuits where the same ground is covered in different walks, instructions are given as if for the first time, so that you do not have to turn pages back and forth. I hope that you will find, as I did, an added pleasure in completing two or three walks in one area. Returning to the same lovely village to start another walk is like returning to a well loved picture: to walk out from it in another direction is like discovering another painting by the same artist.

Preface

The Route Maps at the beginning of each walk are designed to give you a picture of the 'shape' of the route, so that you can see at a glance the possibilities of variations you might choose, and of the connections with other walks in the section.

The Strip Maps are a simplified version of the route maps. They go UP the page, as if they were unfolding under your feet. (Your next destination, not necessarily north, is at the top of the page.) They are intended to clarify the instructions and illustrate the words.

Maps With the instructions and maps given in this book you should not need any other maps: but a dedicated walker usually finds it comforting and interesting to have an OS map handy. The relevant ORDNANCE SURVEY MAPS for this area are:
Landranger 141 (with a tiny overflow into Landranger 130/140) and Pathfinder maps SK60/70, 80/90, 61/71 and SP69/79, 89 (plus a tiny bit of SP 68/78).

Distances Given for walks in the text are approximations, measured by rule of thumb. (A good rambler's thumb measures one mile on OS Pathfinder maps. For increased accuracy, miles can be measured in knots, with a piece of string knotted at mile intervals, using the scale on the map!) For smaller distances I refer to yards, although I know this is an archaic measure. One yard equals one good rambler's stride. The reader can of course make more accurate computations using a fine mapping ruler, but for most purposes the kind of measurement given here is perfectly adequate to give you an idea of what time you need to allow, how much energy you will need and at what point you need to look out for stiles or other crossing places.

The Time Required for a walk depends on your pace, but a rough guide is to allow an hour for every two miles. The shorter walks in this book might take a summer afternoon or evening. In the winter it might be advisable to set off in the morning. If you join two walks together you will need to make a day of it.

Planning Your Route An evening spent reading about the walk and looking at the maps might be time well spent, especially if you are not sure of your walking capacity. If you plan to join walks together it might be advisable to make a note in the text as a reminder.

Clothing and Equipment Strong, comfortable waterproof shoes or boots and a rucsac or pack for a waterproof jacket (if only to sit on at intervals!) and some emergency food and drink are all the equipment you really need. This countryside is not usually in the whistle-and-compass league (though I must confess that I always carry them!).

Car Parking You need to park with discretion and consideration in small villages. The roads are often narrow and needed for large farming vehicles. There is often space near the church or it may be possible to ask the landlord if you can park in the pub yard.

Accommodation and Refreshment Suggestions will be found in the introductions to each section.

Introduction to East Leicestershire

General Introduction Each of the walks in this book will receive its own introduction so that you can read about the places you pass through and perhaps stop if you wish to savour these beautiful little towns and villages. But it is perhaps appropriate here to describe a few general features of the whole area.

The Area If you have the OS Landranger map 141 (Kettering and Corby) you will see that almost all the walks in this book are in the top half of that map. The part of East Leicestershire covered by these walks extends from Foxton Locks and Saddington in the west (south of Leicester) to Rutland Water, due east of Leicester and close to Oakham and Uppingham. The most northerly point is Burton Lazars, near Melton Mowbray (just off the 141 map), and our southernmost points are Foxton and Welham, which is on the river Welland, Leicesteshire's County Boundary with Northamptonshire.

The A47 cuts straight across the middle. The rivers, too, run mainly west and east, most of them starting near Tilton, where 7 streams are said to originate. The rivers Gwash and Chater (which are really only little streams) flow into Rutland Water. The Eyebrook goes through Eyebrook reservoir and then joins the River Welland. Minor streams drain south into the Welland valley, where there is lush cattle pasture.

The Landscape Our walks take to the high ground, mainly in rolling grassland country five or six hundred feet up, with occasional spinneys and clumps of trees punctuating the skyline. We descend gradually to cross the shallow little streams. It is gentle countryside but you will not, I think, have reason to complain that Leicestershire is flat!

"Over these fields the winter wind flows uninterrupted like a sea and there is no shelter but near the thin and bony spinneys...". (Hoskins)

Its History The area is rich in history and abundant in lovely churches and stately homes and the routes we take are often the ancient ways of long distance paths connecting small settlements with the great religious centres or important market and trading places.

The Footpaths are varied but mainly follow old trackways. We walk along part of the old Bronze Age Jurassic Way (which Hoskins traces across Leicestershire along the high ground from Husbands Bosworth, through Kibworth, Three Gates, Rolleston Lodge, Tilton and on towards Somerby and Burrough Hill).

These ancient routes developed into the old pack horse tracks, and were used by later generations. Some, of course, became roads. Even the Romans who were such determined road makers did not always scorn the tracks made by their precursors. The same routes were used by the 5th century Germanic invaders and the later Scandinavians settled beside them. The paths have been used by generations of footwalkers travelling through these little villages.

Placenames The place names of the villages of Leicestershire have a story to tell mainly of the Anglo Saxons and Danes who started invading and settling here after the

Romans left in about 400 A.D. The significant feature of Leicestershire is the network of small villages settled by the Germanic and Scandinavian tribes in the post-Roman period. The upland fields we cross in our walks were once part of the Danelaw (established by the Danish invaders in the 9th century). By the time the Danes arrived the Anglo Saxons had already settled in the more sheltered spots (like Billesdon, Rolleston and Nosely). The newcomers were left out in the cold and windy uplands (around Frisby and Gaulby, Illston and Carlton). The place name endings still show this.

Anglosaxon Placename Endings

The AngloSaxon placename endings are: -ton, field, worth and ham. We find examples of these in WigsTON and ThurmasTON (where the earliest Anglo Saxon cemeteries are found, quite close to the Roman town of Leicester), MareFIELD, KibWORTH and WelHAM, OakHAM and EmpingHAM (where there was an important 6th century burial ground). These are very early AngloSaxon settlements.

Other AngloSaxon placenames in our area are: GLOOS-TON (Glor's tun), HALLATON (tun in a narrow valley), East, West and Church LANGTON (Old English lang tun, long village). (TUR LANGTON was originally Turlington (the tun of Tyrli's people), but became changed to Tur Langton by analogy with the neighbouring Langtons) BILLESDON (Bil's dun), TILTON (Tila's tun) and ROLLESTON (Hrolf's tun or Hrothwulf's tun. .)

Scandinavian Placename Endings are:

-by, toft, thorpe and we find examples of these in: TugBY, LowesBY, IngarsBY, ScrapTOFT, OTHORPE and THORPE Langton.

The Viking raiders overran the Midlands in about 877 A.D. English rule was not re-established until King Alfred's time in about 896 A.D. During this time many AngloSaxon settlements acquired a Danish prefix: CROXton HUNGAR-ton ROLLESton (Hrolf or Hrothwulf may be the name of a Norseman) so we get an interesting combination of Germanic and Scandinavian place names. And some AngloSaxon names acquired a Scandinavian pronunciation (thus Sheffington, Sceaftinga's tun, became Skeffington, and Charlton became Carlton).

Other Scandinavian names in the area are:

INGARSBY (Old Norse or Old Danish Ingvar's by), WELSH MYERS (Old Norse myrr, a marsh or bog), LOWESBY (Old Scandinavian lausa, a slope), TUGBY (Scandinavian Toki's by), NOSELY (Northwulf's Leah), ILLSTON (Old Norse Iolf's tun).

Many places in the area acquired an additional nametag after the Norman Conquest, when Norman families gained possession and built great houses: thus we have:

Stonton WYVILLE (Stantone) held by the Norman family, de Wyville 1209-35, CARLTON CURLIEU (the churl's town) held by the Curly family in 1270 and NEVILLE Holt named after the Neville family.

Most of the place names of villages were thus fixed soon after the Norman Conquest and for interesting new additions you need to look to the names of spinneys or coverts (like Botany Bay, named when the Colonies were in the news) or farms and houses which sometimes change their names according to fashion (like Moscow farm near Burrough Hill or America Lodge near Neville Holt).

For these later names you might like to do your own research! It is always interesting to find out why people name their houses so! Is it a name they inherited? does it describe some natural feature? or is it a version of their own name? If the answer is yes, then they are continuing an old tradition.

The Sites
We pass through Iron Age Hill Forts, (Burrough), Roman settlements (like Medbourne), ancient Religious sites and places of pilgrimage (like Wing maze) and remains of old forests (Leighfield and Rockingham). We pass a Norman motte and bailey castle site (Hallaton) and go through former medieval deer parks (Lyddington and Stockerston). We pass close to stately homes (like Quenby) in lovely parkland (like Lowesby) which formerly belonged to families who played a significant part in national history (like the Digby and Hazelrigg families).

Some of the villages we go through were once important resting places on routes to major settlements, (Ingarsby and Illston on the Hill) or on the bishop's touring route (like Lyddington Bishop's Palace). Some of them remained important and were provided with beautiful stone churches, landmarks for us and places of worship for small communities (Hallaton and Tilton). Others have long since disappeared and are now marked only by placenames, a remaining Manor House and humps and hollows in pasture fields (Ingarsby, Quenby, Nosely).

History on the Ground
The trained eye can see evidence on the ground of old farming patterns where the ridge and furrows in our pasture fields show us that in medieval times these fields were ploughed and where disturbances in the ground show us that there were once buildings here.

We can also note the tell-tale marks where in more recent times hedges and tree lines have been removed and we pass ruins of old farmhouses in the fields, where once whole families lived and worked. Now of course we can walk for a whole day and see no one working in the fields, apart from the earmuffed tractor driver in the distance ploughing a lonely furrow or spreading chemical fertilizers!

The traffic too has gone from the old railway lines and canals, with tunnels and viaducts now unused and abandoned. You might hear the noise of motor vehicles as you approach the main Leicester-Uppingham road but for the most part your walking will be away from the sound of traffic or industry. The loudest sounds will probably be the occasional din of low flying aircraft in Rutland. For the rest, this is peaceful countryside.

The Landscape Foxes and Farmland
This is of course fox hunting country. Our great modern historian of the Leicestershire countryside, W.G.Hoskins, reconciled me to that fact when he pointed out that the protection of our trees and hedges has perhaps been due to the popularity of fox hunting among Leicestershire land owners!

(Speaking as one who has walked alone over the hills near Hallaton with a fox walking in front of me like a dog, slowly and companionably, I must say that I am nevertheless one who cheers the fox and omits to tell the hunt which way I saw it go!)

You are likely to see foxes and horses in most of the walks described. In autumn and winter you are likely to see the hunt. The main Hunts in Leicestershire are the Belvoir, Cottesmore, Fernie, Pytchley and Quorn. This is Fernie country.

It is also farming country. Ridges and furrows in our

pasture fields and around our lost villages show that the land has long been cultivated. (They are made by the ploughs turning earth over to one side as they progress round the strips of farmed land, like allotment strips.) But, by an irony of history, the land which was for so long pasture is now turned over to arable, ploughed land. Old paths which went directly from village to village over pasture fields are now obstructed by crops.

Footpaths and the Law
Technically these paths should be reinstated by rolling or left unploughed. Paths which go beside hedges are headland paths and it is an offence to plough these at all. But farmers in this area have for many years broken the law, and got away with it. I am afraid that despite increased concern over the preservation of public rights of way and despite increased action on the part of the County Council to prosecute lawbreaking landowners you will find some paths in these walks obstructed by crops at some seasons.

Our Routes
The paths selected for this book are not usually obstructed, and wherever possible I've chosen well marked tracks and clearly visible routes. I have tried to avoid roadwalking altogether, as country roads seem to be as dangerous as motorways now. But there are several points where you will need to cross over the main A47 Uppingham road. Our final walk takes us into Rutland, where there still seem to be more horses than people, and of course to Rutland Water, where a modern water supply manages to be a tourist attraction and a haven for wild life.

The summer of 1988 was for me a marvellous summer spent in walking these routes, selecting the prettiest and the most varied and interesting for you. I hope that you enjoy them as much as I do!

Heather MacDermid

Contents: from Foxton Locks to Rutland Water

CONTENTS

STEP 1. Foxton Locks
Two walks which could be linked into a longer figure of eight walk.

Mainly easy track, including some canal towpath.

The walk could also be started from Saddington or Fleckney, using the headings provided.

A lovely canal circuit. Our walk goes OVER the canal tunnel, so we don't have to "leg" our way through, as bargees did in the past. We take the pleasant route provided for the horses.

For the long figure of eight walk of 14 miles you need to insert the second walk into the first one when you reach Smeeton Westerby. Follow instructions for walk 2 when you reach Smeeton Westerby church and then return to walk 1 instructions to complete the figure of eight. (This requires a bit of ingenuity! Perhaps you'd better do the separate circuits first!)

STEP 2. Keyham
Two 4 mile walks, starting from Keyham and Ingarsby. The walks can be linked into an 8 mile figure of eight walk crossing through Old Ingarsby.

(The walks could also be started from Houghton on the Hill, which is one mile away by lane from Ingarsby, or from Scraptoft which is one and a half miles away along Covert Lane.)

Crossing the dismantled railway and the deserted village of Ingarsby. The walk begins along a lane and returns beside the stream.

From the deserted village of Ingarsby to the stately home and lost village of Quenby. Returning on the old County road, now a grassy track.

STEP 3. Tilton
A 9 mile walk which can easily be reduced to 6 miles, by omitting a 3 mile circuit which can be done on a separate occasion, starting from Skeffington.

The second walk can be a 9 mile round or it can be added on to the first for a grand figure-of-eight walk of 16 miles.

And there's a short 4 mile stroll suitable for wet or wintry weather, keeping mainly to tracks.

(One of the many charms of this area is the tempting tea place at Halstead, when you finish the walks.

Skeffington pub, The Fox and Hounds, serves excellent meals, too, including vegetarian dishes and, on certain days of the week, fresh fish.)

Contents: from Foxton Locks to Rutland Water

Contents: from Foxton Locks to Rutland Water

STEP 7: Glooston to Tugby via Goadby
A 9 mile figure-of-eight walk which can be done as two separate short circuits starting from Goadby. Goadby is only a small village with no refreshment facilities, but one circuit can be extended a mile to take you through Glooston, which has a pub/restaurant and the other goes through Tugby which has pubs providing good food.

STEP 8. Hallaton
A 6 mile circuit around the beautiful and interesting village of Hallaton. This begins by going towards the Welland valley and then climbs up to the high plateau, with scarcely a building in sight.
Hallaton itself has lovely and interesting buildings, a motte and bailey castle site, a small museum, a duck pond with ducks and a picture book village green. There is a good choice of refreshment stops.

STEP 9. Belton
Three walks of 6, 4 and 8 miles, which can be linked to make an 11 mile figure-of-eight walk or a 15 miler or a 12 miler, starting from Belton. It is possible to eat and drink well at Belton and at Braunston. It is possible to stay in Belton for bed and breakfast.

STEP 10. Burrough Hill

Contents: from Foxton Locks to Rutland Water

STEP 11. Medbourne to Uppingham

A series of walks to take you from Medbourne, near the southern border of the county, to Uppingham in Rutland. The walks can be done as separate circuits or could be linked as one long weekend walk from Medbourne to Uppingham returning after a rest there (10 miles each way). Perhaps you'd like to try the separate circuits first and then try linking them into an impressive longer walk! To do the long walk simply follow the instructions for Medbourne to Blaston, Blaston to Stockerston, Stockerston to Uppingham. Return by following instructions for Uppingham to Lyddington, Lyddington to Stockerston, Stockerston to Blaston and Blaston to Medbourne.

Walk 23. Medbourne • Neville Holt • Blaston

Walk 24. Blaston • Horninghold • Stockerston • Blaston

Uphill and over arable land to begin with then across pasture land with lovely views over the wooded hills, along a quiet road into Uppingham, then following waymarked paths to the historically interesting and entirely beautiful Lyddington in the valley. A choice of road walk to Stoke Dry and beside the Eyebrook reservoir or footpath over high pasture land along an old green lane to descend through the woods to Stockerston.

Shops, refreshments and toilets at Uppingham, a charming little market town.

STEP 12. Rutland Water

Walk 26. Hambleton Peninsula

Walk 27. Manton • Lyndon • Wing • Manton

You need to plan ahead to do this walk and allow time to receive permission to walk a short stretch of path near Manton. This requirement might eventually be relaxed but meanwhile write to Anglia Water Authority, Oundle for permission to pass through the nature reserve at Rutland Water. The walk is worth the trouble involved, though the footpaths between Lyndon and Wing are not always well kept or waymarked.

Foxton Locks

Foxton Locks Foxton Locks lie at a junction of the Grand Union Canal near Market Harborough. At this point the canal has to change level to continue to Welford and Crick on much higher ground.

The Harborough Arm of the canal (which ends in a wharf at Market Harborough) was built in 1805-1809 but the locks to the high ground were not built until 1808 and not finished until 1814.

Going through this staircase of ten locks was a slow process (taking about an hour) and the inclined plane was built and opened in April 1900 as a quicker alternative way of transporting the boats between the two levels. (This could take as little as 7 or 8 minutes.)

The plane has recently been cleared and there are museum facilities in the old Engine house, so it is now easy to see how the system worked although the great engine has been dismantled.

In general terms, the plane consisted of a ramp with runners for two 'baths' into which the long narrow boats could be floated, one at the top level and one at the lower level. The engine could then be used to maximum effect, using one boat 'bath' as a counterweight for the other, as one ascended the runners and one descended.

If you climb up from the Market Harborough arm at the foot of the plane you can see how boats were loaded into their 'baths' and you can then make your way up to the top to see how the runners led to the engine house and were then taken along the high ground to a lock gate where they could be opened up into an arm of canal (now dry). You can

walk along it to see how it connects into the high canal at a fork further along. It was a tremendous undertaking and a very expensive one. It took three years to build and was dismantled in 1911 after only eleven years of use because of insufficient traffic.

Foxton Village The village of Foxton straddles the Market Harborough arm of the canal. The highest part of the village contains the church and manor house and one pub. The school is on the other side of the canal (and is now used as a field centre).

Smeeton Westerby is really a union of two small hamlets. (John Prior's map marks two windmills there in 1777). Westerby is the western settlement of Smee (Smith)'s tun. The little church was built in 1851. The triangular patch of ground below road level near the church is called Pitt gardens and was probably an old gravel pit.

(The story about the village mill that once stood about half a mile west of Smeeton, just south of Mill lane is that it blew down in about 1885, with the miller inside it!)

Debdale Wharf was an important coal wharf. It was the terminus of the canal from 1797 until the Harborough Arm of the canal was built in 1805.

Fleckney Tunnel (also called Saddington tunnel on some maps) was built in 1797 when many fossils were found. The tunnel is about half a mile long. The horse drawn boats were unhitched and while the horses were led over the towpath route above the tunnel, the poor bargees were obliged to 'leg' their boats by lying on the decks and 'walking' along the tunnel to propel the boat to the far end of the tunnel.

Gumley (A Scandinavian place name, variously written as Godmundeslaech 749 Godmundesleah 779 Guthmunde-lai 1147).
The church was rebuilt in 1759. The woods are one of Hanbury's plantations (See the notes on Church Langton for further details). The Hall, built by Joseph Cradock (a friend of Dr Johnson and the actor Garrick), was begun in 1764 and had a private theatre. Only the stable block now remains. Cradock spared no expense on the house but had to sell it and died modestly aged 84.
Arthur Mee (*The Kings England*) describes Gumley as the prettiest village in the county, with its steep hills and dales.

Saddington has a 700 year old church, (restored when it had fallen into a derelict state), with a 14th century tower. The village stands up high in a beautiful position overlooking the 50 acre reservoir.

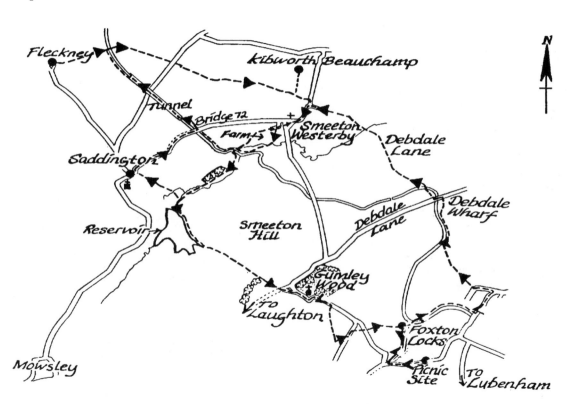

FOXTON LOCKS • FOXTON
• DEBDALE WHARF
• SMEETON WESTERBY
• SADDINGTON RESERVOIR
• GUMLEY • FOXTON LOCKS

$8\frac{1}{2}$ miles, mainly track, some canal towpath and short stretches of road walking through charming villages. It is possible to make a short extension to go into Saddington village for refreshment and there is a shop and tea place at Foxton Locks. There are pubs at Gumley and Foxton.

Foxton is just off the A6 on the Leicester side of Market Harborough. Foxton Locks picnic site is just beyond the village, half way along the road between Foxton village and Gumley and well signposted. It has a good car park and makes a useful start to the walk.

From Foxton Picnic Site turn left and walk along the pedestrian way beside the road to Gumley until you reach the canal. There is a clover leaf route which leads you under the bridge and across a curved wooden footbridge so that you turn right and walk with the canal on your right.

Very soon you come to the top of the famous flight of locks which make a staircase for narrow boats to travel between the high canal and the lower Market Harborough arm. Beyond it to your right is the inclined plane which is equally interesting.

You could leave your exploration of that until the end of the walk, when you celebrate at the cafe with a good pot of tea.

Pass Foxton Bottom lock and walk with the canal still on your right, as if towards Leicester, until you reach the bridge, which you need to cross and then turn back on yourself to walk with the canal on your right again, towards Market Harborough.

Pass the big canal basin and continue to a gap in the hedge on your left just before the next canal bridge. Turn left here and walk along the lane which is parallel to the canal on your right. At the road we need to turn left. (The Black Horse pub and the church are to your right up the hill. The Shoulder of Mutton pub is further down the road, on your left).

Where the road swings right at the bottom end of the village, you need to turn left and walk along the lane Unsuitable for Motors. When the lane bends left, turn into the field by the bridleway sign.

You now need to walk slightly away from the stream on your left and keep parallel with the hedge which is some way over to your right. You need to keep in this direction, aiming for the yellow topped marker posts at the end of a hedge ahead of you and then go slightly right moving uphill. Pass a little pond on your right and go to the top corner of the field where the trees edge the canal.

(If the way is obstructed by crops you might need to follow the stream

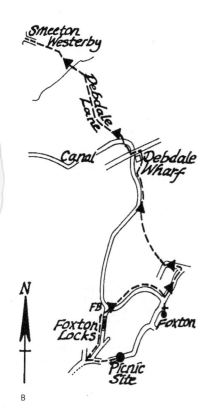

and then turn right to meet the marker post in the hedge.
This route is often well trodden by horses.)
Beyond a little rise in the top corner of the field (where you get fine views over to Gumley and back to Foxton and Gartree prison) you descend to a handgate which leads into a lovely little green lane beside the canal on your left.
Go through the little bridlegate at the end of the lane and continue with the hedge bordering the canal uphill on your left and go through the next little bit of green lane.
Then swing right to reach the corner of the hedge which juts out in front of you.
Follow this hedge on your left and go through the fence and gate beside Debdale Wharf farmhouse and cattle pens. (If it is obstructed by barbed wire, complain at the house!) There is a footpath sign on the opposite side of the road.
Turn left and walk past the Wharf house and cross the canal bridge.
Turn right and walk along the track, passing Debdale Wharf boatyard with its neatly stacked rows of narrow boats beyond the hedge on your right.

The track (Debdale Lane) leads over another canal bridge and continues, following a hedge on the right, all the way into Smeeton Westerby. When you reach Main street, opposite Blacksmiths Lane, turn left and walk through the village to reach Smeeton Westerby church.
(At this point you can if you wish make a longer walk by inserting the Smeeton Westerby 5 mile walk on page 19. Then continue as follows.)

From Smeeton Westerby Church to Saddington Reservoir When you reach the sunken triangular green at the road junction where the road to Gumley swings left, opposite the church which is on your right, continue between the two roads and walk downhill along the grassy track over the triangular green between a cottage and fenced off garden.
Continue uphill to the road.
Turn left and then immediately right, to keep in the same direction along a little jitty between red brick walls.
Turn left when you meet the lane.
Continue to the end of the lane and cross the fence.
Keep in the same direction down the open field making for a di-pole power line on the hill in the next field. Cross

the footbridge over the stream and swing left to pass the di-pole on your right. (Ignore the track on your left which goes up to cross a canal bridge on your left.) Go through the gate on the right and continue with the stream on your left. Follow the path which goes under the high arch of the aquaduct.

The map indicates that you should turn left immediately you have crossed under the canal (although most people go straight on at this point, following the track and crossing the wooden cartbridge). If you turn left you need to weave your way on high ground through a rather wet piece of woodland just below the canal and then swing downhill to your right to walk beside some sharp meanders of the old stream bed.

The path now goes along a lovely pasture valley, with the stream and woodland on your right and a canal feeder stream up on your left. These come close together at the end of the field. Cross the fence and continue close to the feeder stream on your left. Smeeton hill rises on your left and Saddington village is on the hill on your right.

(If you wish to visit Saddington village you can turn right here and

cross two white railed wooden footbridges. Continue uphill in the same direction to meet the road. The path is waymarked as it is part of the Leicestershire Round. Turn left along the road to reach the very pleasant pub with a garden overlooking the reservoir. The church sometimes does Sunday teas in summer. Return by the same route to continue the walk to Saddington reservoir.)

If you do not wish to go into Saddington village, continue close to the feeder stream. Cross the little weir and the footbridge and go up the bank to join the lane. Turn left along the lane and pass Saddington reservoir on your right.

This track takes you to Gumley. A steepish climb at the end of the hollow way leads to the main road and lovely views. Continue straight ahead on the road signposted to Gumley (0.5 mile).

A path on your left leads through a kissing gate to the church, where you need to turn right to rejoin the road at a sharp bend. (But if you prefer to see the Victorian weighbridge, keep on the road. You will see it on your right.)

From Gumley to Foxton Locks, walk down the main street of Gumley, passing first the stables of the old Gumley Hall and then the old Engine House on your left. Near the telephone box and post box on your left there is a footpath sign on each side of the road.

Take the footpath on your right, which leads between brick walls of houses up an ashphalt track to a fence at the top. In the field go diagonally left to pass the corner of a field which juts out.

Follow the power lines downhill, moving slightly away from the hedge on your left. The true crossing over the stream is at a little bend, in line with the top corner of field ahead of you, but it is usually obstructed and you may find it best to go to the gate in the bottom left corner of the field.

Cross the stream and go through the gate in the left corner of the next field. Turn left and walk along the road for 100 yards. Turn right to cross the fence at the footpath sign. (This cuts off a little corner of the road.) Walk parallel with the stream on your right and cross the road. Go through the handgate and keep in the same general direction walking with a hedge on your left.

The flight of Foxton locks is now ahead of you and the engine house and the top lock house can be clearly seen.

Make your way down to a metal gate in the far bottom right corner of the field and go over the bridge to the foot of the locks.

Now is the time to see if the cafe is

open and to explore the inclined plane, the engine house and museum. If you are not too tired, it's fascinating to wander over the site and to work out how the boats were brought up and down from the Market Harborough arm to the high Grand Union line via the inclined plane and the link canal basin.

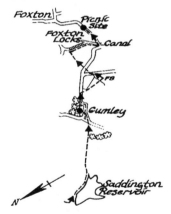

The picnic site car park is at the top of the flight of locks. Turn left along the road and it is on your right.

Walk 2 – Foxton   •   Smeeton Westerby

SMEETON WESTERBY •
CANAL • FLECKNEY TUNNEL •
SMEETON WESTERBY

This short walk of $5\frac{1}{2}$ miles could be
started at Saddington, which would
add $1\frac{1}{2}$ miles to the walk or from
Fleckney, which would add 1 mile
or from Kibworth, which is less
than a mile away from
Smeeton Westerby.
If you start from Smeeton Westerby
you can choose to add on the short
stretch of road walk into Saddington, less than a mile each way, to
see the village and have a drink
overlooking the reservoir. This
would make it a $7\frac{1}{2}$ mile walk.
You could make this a longer walk
by inserting it into the Foxton-
Saddington reservoir walk (which
goes through Smeeton Westerby) to
make a 14 mile figure of eight.

1. From Smeeton Westerby Church
to the Canal Turn into the Gumley
road for a few yards and then turn
right to walk along the green path

between Ivy Cottage on your left
and gardens on your right in the
triangular green in the road
junction opposite the church.
At the top of the hill cross the road
and move slightly left and then
immediately right to walk in the
same direction along the little jitty
which goes between red brick
walls opposite you.
Turn left at the road. At Smeeton
farmhouse the road swings right.
Pass the bungalow and turn left
through the farm gate just before
Westerby farmhouse.
Walk downhill along the green
track between the shrub hedges of
the gardens on each side. Move
slightly right in the field, passing a
pond on your left, and cross the
gate and bridge over the stream.
(The barbed wire here is an
illegal obstruction!)
Continue moving right, passing
between the stream on your right
and a spinney on your left, making
your way uphill to the far left
corner of the field, where a gate

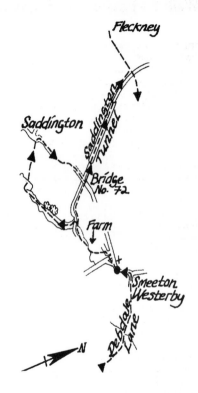

Walk 2 – Foxton • Smeeton Westerby

brings you out close to the canal at the top of the hill. (We are going to continue in the same direction, walking along the canal.)
To reach the canal towpath you need to cross the fence at the right of the canal bridge and make your way down to the canal. Turn right and walk with the canal on your left. This is a very pretty stretch of canal, with a pool frequented by herons beyond a bend in the canal, but you need to watch the towpath as it is a bit fragile here.
To continue on the Smeeton Westerby circuit keep following the canal to reach the Fleckney tunnel as in section 2 and 3.

2. From Canal Bridge No. 72 to Fleckney Tunnel
Walk along the towpath with the canal on your left. Fleckney tunnel is ahead of you and the newly gravelled path goes uphill over the tunnel. The green lane leads you above the canal, through which so many boats were pushed by "legging" while the horses went along the path we now take.

The tunnel is about $\frac{1}{2}$ mile long, The path crosses the Kibworth-Saddington road and continues as a pretty green lane, emerging spectacularly at the tunnel end, where you swing left to walk along the towpath with the canal on your right.
Pass under the next bridge and after 20 yards turn left through a handgate. Turn left again to meet the bridge over the canal.
(If you start from Fleckney take the path to Smeeton Westerby which begins at the end of the little cul de sac on Kibworth Lane. Walk in a straight line to meet this bridge over the canal.)

3. From Fleckney Bridge to Smeeton Westerby
Cross the bridge over the canal. Walk uphill along the well marked path, with the hedge on your left and go through the hand gate ahead of you in the top corner of the field. Go through the first gate and walk parallel with the hedge (100 yards away from you) on your left in this big open field. (Beyond this hedge

is the forest of electicity poles of the sub-station.)

Meet a handgate in the jutting out corner of the next field. Continue on the well marked track to reach the Saddington-Kibworth road at the footpath sign.

Cross to the lane opposite and continue along it all the way into Smeeton Westerby. (This is a beautiful lane in good weather, but can be muddy in winter.) When you reach the first house the lane becomes a surfaced road (Mill Lane). As you approach the village of Smeeton your route is crossed by the signposted path from Kibworth Beauchamp, just a few fields away to your left.

Kibworth walkers can join the walk here, coming from Kibworth on the well marked and signposted path to Smeeton Westerby.)
The Kibworth path crosses the lane and continues as a pretty way straight to Smeeton Westerby church but the village deserves a visit, even though it has very few facilities (a telephone box but no shops). To see the village ignore the footpath signs and continue along Mill Lane.

Turn right at the Kings Head pub, pass the village hall on your left and continue through the village street until you reach the road junction to Foxton and Gumley near Smeeton Westerby church, where the walk began.

4. From Saddington Village to Canal Bridge 72 (1 mile). If you wish to start from Saddington Village
walk towards Smeeton Westerby, passing Saddington church and pub on your right. This road, which used to be a gated road and which still has remains of cattle grids and gate posts, has delightful views over the area to be walked and of the hills beyond. On a clear day you can see over to Church Langton and Billesdon and Tilton. The canal lies at the foot of the hill, with Fleckney tunnel to your left. This is your next goal. Beyond it on the skyline is the line of the green lane we will be taking to Smeeton Westerby.

Cross the road bridge (canal bridge no 72) and turn left to walk along the canal.
(Saddington walkers now walk sections 2, 3, 1 and 5.)

5. To Saddington from Canal Bridge No. 72 (1 mile). Leave the
canal at the first bridge (no. 72). Climb up to the road and turn left. This road goes uphill all the way into Saddington. If you walk on the little foot track in the grass verge on your left you have fine views over to Saddington reservoir below you. You can also trace the whole route of this walk! A very satisfying experience! (And on Sundays in summer you can perhaps have tea in Saddington village.)
Return from Saddington to canal bridge no. 72 as in section 4.
A most beautiful circuit in canal country.

Quenby Hall

Keyham A small village on the outskirts of Leicester just beyond Scraptoft. It is marked as part of the King's Manor on Domesday map, spelt Caiham. (On John Prior's map of 1777 it is spelt as Keam.) It now has few claims to fame, but hit the headlines in 1762 when a terrible fire raged there.

Nicholls notes particularly the impressive longevity of the inhabitants, with people living to the great ages of 70, 80, and 92 or 3. "There is something marvellous in these instances of great age".

Around 1800 there was in the village a boarding school for between 50 and 60 boarders, who "on Sundays make a very pleasing appearance at church among the rustic worshippers. They occupy the chancel, where they appear like beds of lilies in a flower garden". (Nicholls III p. 879)

Ingarsby is a deserted village site, well documented by Hoskins, who maps the site so that we can detect where each street lay. The plan can be clearly seen on the ground, especially when the sun is low in the sky. The best view is probably from Monk's grave, the mound at the end of Covert Lane. Ingarsby was finally depopulated by Leicester Abbey, the owners of the land, in 1469. It is interesting to read from Sir Thomas More's UTOPIA (1516) a passage critical of landowners in depopulations like this.....

For look, in what parts of the realm doth grow the finest and therefore dearest wool, ther noblemen and gentlemen, yea and certain abbots, holy men no doubt, not contenting themselves with the yearly revenues and profits that were wont to grow to the forefathers and predecessors of their lands, nor being content that they live in rest and pleasure.....; they inclose all into pastures; they throw down houses; they pluck down towns, and leave nothing standing but only the church - to make of it a sheep house. ....those good holy men turn all dwelling places and all glebeland into desolation and wilderness.

Ingarsby Old Hall was built at the time of the depopulation, about 1470 but was enlarged in Elizabethan times (1579) and refronted in 1706. The gardens are sometimes opened to the public for charity.

The Railway line, now dismantled, came through a tunnel which passes under Covert Lane, where the air vent can still be seen. The end of this has now been closed. Ingarsby village still boasts a fine old Station Masters house.

Monks Grave Little is known of this mound. It seems too small for a motte or a windmill site. It could be a moated or fenced off rabbit warren from a time when rabbits were precious food. But why it should have acquired the name of Monks Grave is a mystery. (It does of course lie on the track from Leicester Abbey to Launde Abbey but who the monk was or why he should be buried here no one seems to know.)

Quenby about 7 miles north east of Leicester. The name is a Scandinavianised form. It appears in Domesday Book as Queneberie from the Old English Cwene burg, the queen's manor, but the 'burg' was later spelt 'by' as in so many of the Danish settlements hereabouts.

(Compare this with Queniborough, which has kept its AngloSaxon ending.) I wonder which queen it was named after and whether the Danes did take over her manor, or whether the name just changed by analogy with the other Scandinavian villages.

This is another lost village, superseded by a stately house. It was depopulated in the late 15th century and the great Jacobean house (built for George Ashby) was constructed in 1621-36. The house has remarkable diaper brick patterning and a ha ha wall round the garden. (Ha ha walls and ditches were popular in the 18th century landscaping of great houses, so that the view, with cattle and sheep picturesquely distanced, could be left uninterrupted by walls and fences while the gardens could be protected from the unwelcome attentions of animals.)

Nicholls tells us (vol III.1 p295) that the house was in the possession of the Ashby family from 1247. Anne Skevington, daughter and heir of William Ashby, died in 1536. Her son Ashby married Mary, heir of Eusby Shukburgh of Naseby 1652, thus uniting the arms of Shukburgh and Ashby.

About 1700 George Ashby planted nine fine Cedars, specially imported from Turkey, in the grounds. "These fine trees were in flourishing condition when Mr Shukburgh Ashby came to the estate but, being blocked up by other trees from sight, he laid them open to view: which they took so ill, that they immediately died". (All was not absolutely lost; the timber was later used in restoring Hungarton chapel.)

This Mr Shukburgh Ashby, of Blaby, was born in 1724. : "a gentleman of first rate moral and literary attainments, who made a new village of cottages in Hungarton." He was not in direct line of succession to the house but purchased the estate in 1759 and immediately embarked on ambitious plans for restoring the house and the neighbouring village of Hungarton. (When you go through the village of Hungarton you can see all the houses dated 1760-1770.) He became M.P. for Leicester in 1784, died in 1792 and was buried at Hungarton.

In an anonymous book 'The Beauties of England and Wales: Leicestershire' (written by Britton?) published 1815 the author tells us that when Shuckbrough Ashby acquired it (1760-1770) he "found the house a mere shell, much out of repair and the offices in ruin. He has, in a few years, brought the whole into complete order, fitted up all the rooms in a state of great propriety.... his library superbly filled with the best and most expensive books, in several languages. Around the house is a new terrace which commands a great variety of prospect; on one side very extensive, over a distant hilly country, and even to the mountains of the peak. On the other side a beautiful landscape of hanging hills, with scattered woods, shelving into a winding valley, so low that you look down on upon it in a very picturesque manner; the sides of the hills all cut into rich inclosures."

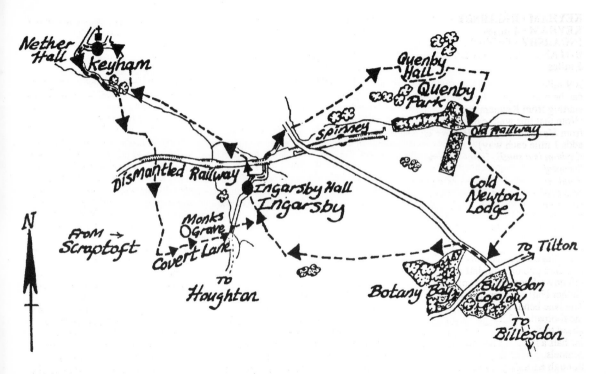

**KEYHAM • INGARSBY •
KEYHAM • 4 miles
INGARSBY • QUENBY HALL •
BOTANY BAY • INGARSBY •
5 miles**

A 9 mile figure of eight walk which can be done as two short walks, starting from Keyham and Ingarsby. (Note that this walk can be started from *Houghton on the Hill* which adds 1 mile each way)
Keyham is a small village beyond Scraptoft, off the A47 Uppingham Road, east of Leicester. Parking can be a problem in the village as the roads are narrow. You could ask at the Dog and Gun for permission to park in their large car park.

From Keyham church walk down the village street, passing the Dog and Gun pub on your left and turn left down Snow's Lane (passing Nether Hall on your right).
The lane bends sharp left. (Ignore the footpaths which go straight ahead to Scraptoft.) Follow the lane for half a mile to Keyham Boarding Kennels. The bridleway goes through a stable yard which has alarming notices about loose dogs and misleading notices about there being No Through road; but press on undaunted. Cross under the power lines and take the left fork along the green lane.
Pass the house on your right and walk between a spinney on your left and the hedge on your right. Two gates at the end of the lane take you across the stream.
Walk with the stream on your right for one field, then turn sharp left to walk close to the hedge on your left until you come to a small triangular spinney on your left just before the field ends. Turn right here and walk uphill with the hedge on your left.
The old red brick railway bridge is in the top corner of this field. There is a crossing in the hedge on your left 100 yards below it. Go through this hedge and turn right to walk up to the railway bridge.
(The old railway line is not a right of way but does make a very attractive short cut to Ingarsby.) Once across the bridge you can see to your left the old hall of Ingarsby with its red brick tower and the old railway houses now painted white. Billesdon Coplow, the wooded hill with its distinctive nick, can be picked out.
Cross the bridge and continue in the same direction for four more fields, where you will meet Covert Lane, the green lane which comes from Scraptoft to Ingarsby.
(In the second field, ignore the two gates on your right. They lead into fields on your right. Go through the narrow neck at the end of this field and walk through a little 'corridor' in the next. When the short stretch of hedge on your right swings away from you, keep straight on to meet the next gate half way along the hedge facing you. The fourth gate leads you onto Covert Lane).
Turn left along Covert lane and walk between hedges to the gate which takes you into an open field.
(This end of Covert Lane is a good place to stop to admire the view. Quenby Hall and Ingarsby Hall nestle in the trees diagonally left. Quenby Hall in the trees on the skyline just to the right of Ingarsby.

Billesdon Coplow is in front of you.)
The path now goes diagonally left across a big undulating pasture field, past a telegraph pole in the middle of the field, to a gate on the skyline between Quenby Hall and Billesdon Coplow.
Stop at the gate to admire the views again before you descend the hill. (From here, especially if the light is right, you can see in the valley ahead of you the humps and hollows of the lost village of Ingarsby, tracing the pattern of the medieval streets and houses.)
Go downhill, along the track which is usually well marked and rutted by vehicles. (On your left is the interesting ditched mound known as Monk's Grave.) Turn left when you reach the Ingarsby lane which comes along the valley from Houghton on the Hill.
(People starting the walk from Houghton can join us here by walking along the Ingarsby Lane.)

Walk across the bridge over the stream and cross the stile beside the first gateway on your right, at the bridleway sign. This leads you up the main street of the lost village of Ingarsby. Pass the pond on your left and walk uphill with a fence over to your left. Aim for the isolated tree on the skyline which grows in the hollow of the "street".
Once past this tree, turn left. Go through the gateway on the left, and walk with the hedge on your right. Walk directly to Ingarsby old hall, ignoring gates on your right.
Emerge at the road, opposite the wall of the hall.
Turn right and pass Ingarsby hall on your left.
At this point you can decide whether to return to Keyham or to add on the next walk which will take you on to Quenby Hall and Botany Bay. If you decide to add on the 5 mile walk, follow the instructions for the next walk and then turn back to this page for the return to Keyham. ($1\frac{1}{2}$ miles)

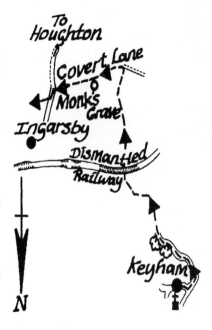

From Ingarsby to Keyham Pass the
hall on your left and turn left at the
footpath sign just beyond the hall.
Weave your way through the farm
sheds, close to the hall for 100 yards
and then sharp right to reach the stile
over the old railway line and thence
down to the stream.

Turn left to walk with the stream on
your right. In 300 yards, cross over
the concrete footbridge and continue
in the same direction but with the
stream now on your left.

The footpath goes in a straight line to
Keyham. You are aiming for a pylon
which can be seen ahead of you. (The
stream winds away to your left but
returns to meet you near the far
corner of the field.)

When you reach the field corner,
cross into the next field and continue
with the stream on your left until you
reach the next crossing point, 50
yards uphill from the stream.

Cross the next narrow field and
continue in the same direction. (The
next field is at present a market
garden and you might need to skirt
the edge of the crops to reach the
fence crossing.)

Continue in the same direction, past a
stable building and through a small
paddock.

At the end of the paddock you need to
go diagonally right to a point beside a
pylon. The field, however, is divided
into small wired paddock areas making
a straight route impossible. Fence
crossings are provided and indicate the
route to enable you to reach the hedge
crossing point, just to the right of
the pylon.

Cross this hedge and then go slightly
left, making for the red brick building
which used to be the Fold Cafe,
Keyham. A newly diverted route takes
you right round the house and garage,
but it is not well kept and the barbed
wire can be hazardous.

Walk along the village street, to reach
the church on your right and the Dog
and Gun on your left.

INGARSBY • QUENBY HALL • BOTANY BAY • INGARSBY • 5 miles

A very pleasant 2 hour stroll over mainly pasture land with gently rolling hills, crossing two lost medieval villages and passing two stately homes and the old LNER railway. What more could a walker desire?

It is difficult to find space to park at Ingarsby, as the lanes are narrow and farm vehicles need to pass, but you may find one suitable layby beside the lane from Houghton, before you reach the stream and footpath sign.

You could start the walk from Houghton and walk along the lane for a mile. You could also start it from the end of Covert Lane, Scraptoft, walking across two fields to join the start at Ingarsby.

From Ingarsby Old Hall walk down Ingarsby Lane (passing footpath signs to Keyham on your left). Go under the railway bridge and pass the 1862 LNER Old Station Master's House on your right.

At this point Hungarton church spire and Quenby Hall stand out on the skyline ahead of you. Your target is Quenby Hall.

Continue down to the T-junction. Cross the road and go through the gate (slightly to your right). Go downhill to cross over the little bridge and then uphill (parallel to the hedge which is about 100 yards to your left) towards Quenby Hall.

Go through the white topped red gate (this is a sign that you are on Quenby Hall land) and continue in the same direction for two more fields. Go through the little white topped red bridle gate which leads you onto the drive to Quenby Hall.

At the drive turn right and walk towards the Hall, swinging right to leave the drive just before you reach the great house. (You are now walking over the lost village of Quenby). The path goes to the right of the hall garden. Go through the bridle gate and walk with the ha ha wall on your left.

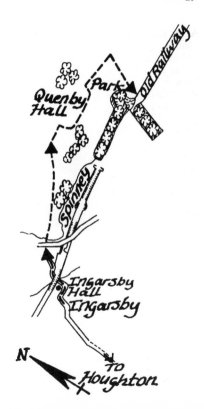

At the end of the wall, swing left to complete your semi circle of the hall and turn right along the drive, which comes from the hall and goes towards Cold Newton.
Walk along the drive passing through one metal gate and then turn right just before the second gate. (This is the D45 path to Cold Newton Lodge.) Walk with the hedge on your left to the first gate and then make your way diagonally right across the field. You are aiming for the bottom right corner of the field, to the left of the wood. (A good marker is the long narrow spinney going uphill in the field ahead. Keep to the left of that.)
A gateway near the bottom corner of the field leads you over the stream and across the old railway line. In the next field follow the hedge on your left and make for the red brick farmhouse of Cold Newton Lodge. There are two gates at the end of the first field a little to the right of the corner. Go through the second of these and walk towards Cold Newton Lodge.
(You cross pretty pasture fields here,

with interesting signs of former habitation. Sludge Hall is the big white house to your left and the wood to your right is Billesdon Coplow.)
Go to the right of Cold Newton Lodge and walk with the hedge on your left for a short distance. Cross the fence ahead of you and turn right to walk along the farm drive. Meet the road near the Billesdon Coplow cross roads.
Turn right and walk along the road for 300 yards (towards Keyham), passing the corner of Botany Bay fox covert. Turn left and go through the gateway.
You are now going to follow the track of the old County road, passing the two "wings" of Botany Bay wood over to your left. It is not marked on OS Pathfinder maps and is not always well marked on the ground but as you walk you will see signs that it is indeed an old road. It goes in a straight line to meet the old lane to Ingarsby lost village. On it you can relax and enjoy the lovely views, knowing that you are walking a route trodden by

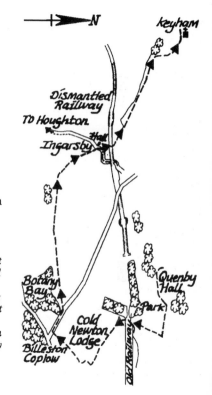

generations of travellers from Launde Abbey to Leicester Abbey via Ingarsby.

In the first field you need to walk towards a line of isolated trees, near the far hedge. Pass Botany Bay wood over to your left. The second field is an open field and you need to keep in the same direction. A line of isolated trees indicates your route, along a slightly raised embankment of ground (signs of an old lane). Meet a hedge on your right and follow it to the corner of the field. In the next field walk with the hedge on your left. In the fourth field continue in the same direction, meet the hedge on your right and walk downhill to the field corner where you go through a gate and join the green lane.

Turn right, pass the pond and walk along the lane. Continue with a hedge on your right until you meet the gate which leads you into the lost village of Ingarsby.

This is a good point to admire the views. Ingarsby Hall is ahead of you. The main" street" of the lost village swings slightly left to join the Ingarsby Lane just to the left of the pond.

(Walkers wishing to return to Houghton on the Hill turn left and walk along Ingarsby Lane.)

To return to Keyham follow the hedge on your right and walk towards Ingarsby Hall. Turn right at the road and follow the instructions on page 28 of the previous walk.

Lowesby Hall

Tilton 10 miles from Leicester, Melton and Uppingham.

The famous historian Nicholls, writing about 1800, says: "Tilton has very rich grazing for sheep and oxen especially on the west and South. On the East about Howbank hill (Robin a Tiptoe), the land is indifferent and very cold insomuch that I am assured by a respectable grazier of the place that snows frequently lie longer upon this land than in the coldest parts of Yorkshire. In the town street is a fine spring. Robin a Tiptoe (also called How back, Houbank), a very steep hill, is 2 miles distant, upon the very top whereof hath been some old Roman fortification, as well may be perceived by the deep trenches and ramparts very eminent upon the South and west side. On the very summit of the hill long ago were planted three trees (ash, I believe) which towered high and threw their branches far and wide. Two of them are now no more and the other is fast going to decay... it was once called Tilton Three Trees. The late Earl of Radnor took considerable pains to have their place supplied with young trees."

The older parts of the Parish church of St Peter are 12th century. (Arthur Mee describes most enthusiastically the gargoyles and says "Heads are everywhere....".) There is a Norman font and tombs of the Digbys who lived here for three centuries. Here lies Sir John Digby of 1269, more than life size and cross legged, in chain mail, fleur de lys on his shield... and his wife Arabella.

The Digbys, who also possessed the manor of Dry Stoke (Stoke Dry), took the name of Tilton, and were known as Dyggeby de Tilton. John de Tilton gave lands at Billesdon and Kirby Bellars to the lepers of St Lazarus de Jerusalem and hence to the brethren of Burton Lazars. He was buried at Tilton.

Later Digbys fought valiantly at the Battle of Bosworth and were rewarded by Henry VII. Everard Greenleaf Digby, who died in 1508 and is buried at Tilton, became steward of Oakham and Uppingham, and High ranger of Lyefield (Leighfield Forest). His wife Jaquetta lies buried at Stoke Dry. (Her will is quoted at length by Nicholls, p 464.)

Another famous Digby, Sir Everard of Gunpowder Plot fame, is not buried at Tilton, because, "being drawn by a false notion of religion, inspired by his unhappy education under Popish priests after his father's death, as Camden says, into the popish plot, was much pitied for that it was his ill fortune to suffer for it being convicted on the 27th Jan 1605 and executed on the 30th at the west end of St Paul's."

Skeffingon though small, is a village of great interest. The little church of St Thomas a Beckett was founded pre-1213 when Edmond of London was appointed priest.

The place name indicates that it is an Anglo Saxon settlement: the 'tun' of Sceaft's people. But the pronunciation and modern spelling indicate that the name has been Scandinavianised.

(In Danelaw areas the 'Scea' parts of words become 'sk' as in Skeffington: in southern parts of England the initial sound becomes softened to 'Sh' as in Shaftesbury, Shipton and Shelton.)

Leicestershire place names are interesting as we are on the borderline between former Danelaw country and the Anglo-Saxon south. The 'by' endings to our village place names indicate Scandinavian settlements, as do endings like 'thorpe' and 'toft'. But these are often combined with the earlier Anglo Saxon names showing perhaps that both communities coexisted peacefully in Leicestershire or that the Danes took over Anglo-Saxon settlements.

The Skeffington family took its name from the place. Sir William Skeffington (1460-1535) was nicknamed 'The Gunner' because of his success in subduing several Irish rebellions against the king. His son, Sir Leonard, was Lieutenant of the Tower of London and devised a torture instrument for use in extracting confessions. This terrible piece of equipment was named 'Skeffington's Maiden'.

Another Skeffington, Sir Thomas, was High Sherriff of Leicestershire. In 1588 he was responsible for mustering 12,500 men between the ages of eighteen and fifty, capable of bearing arms. 2,000 of these joined the army at Tilbury: the rest were sent home to practise with their weapons, to be called upon when needed.

Their Tudor manor house boasts a 'ghost', a grey lady, the last of the Skeffingtons. Masters of the Hunt have lived here and Reynoldstown, winner of the Grand National in 1935 and 1936, was stabled at Skeffington Hall. The stables are known as Reynoldstown stables.

Skeffington Wood was a refuge for villagers during the plague of 1665. Forty three villagers died of the plague between July and November.

The woods were decimated during the war but replanted in 1945-6 by Mr Harry Walker of Syston. There is a monument in the woods recording this fact.

Halstead the highest hamlet in the county, 700 feet above sea level. The hill probably remained above the icecap of Britain in the Ice Age. It serves as a signpost along an ancient trackway, possibly used in the Bronze Age.

Halstead formerly belonged to Launde Abbey. In Domesday Book it is described as part of the Royal Manor of Rodelei (Rothley). When Everard Digby was attainted of High Treason in 1465-6 King Edward 1V gave this land to Sir Walter Devereux.

It may be that a leper colony existed at Halstead farmhouse, where teas are now served. Tilton hospital, which may have been here, is recorded as being given to the Burton Lazar hospital by William Burdett, and Sir John Digby de Tilton gave land to the same cause "for the health of his owne and his ancestors soules" in the 12th century.

Lowesby is another depopulated village. The lost village, deserted in 1487, is in the parkland to the east of the hall. (The rather more spectacular site of Cold Newton lost village is only one mile away.)

Lowesby hall is an Early Georgian brick mansion (at present owned by David Wilson the builder) and the fine gardens are sometimes open to the public. There was an earlier house 1650 bought by Col Hutchinson, governor of Nottingham in Civil war, and sold to Richard Wollaston who died in 1691.

Lowesby church is 13th century. The church gateway arch informs us that from this tiny village 'For King and Country 1914-1918 there died a colonel, a sergeant and three private soldiers...R.I.P.' The little village school, closed in 1969, is now a private house.

Marefield is now only a tiny hamlet with a donkey stud farm. Before 1500 there was a North Marefield, which is now simply a large site of bumps and hollows in the fields, crossed by the footpath from Owston.

Twyford, the parish church of St Andrews has a 12th century north arcade and a gipsy king was buried in 1826 by the churchyard wall.

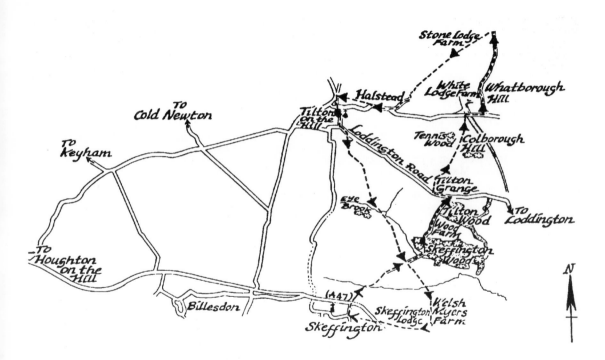

Walk 5 – Tilton

TILTON · WELSH MYERS · SKEFFINGTON · SKEFFINGTON WOOD · STONE LODGE · HALSTEAD · TILTON ·

A delightful (but somewhat tricky) 9 mile walk through the lovely wooded and hilly area around Tilton. (Make a day of it to savour it to the full. Picnic in the woods or eat at Skeffington pub.)
It is possible to shorten it to a 6 mile walk by omitting Skeffington and turning left to go through Skeffington Wood. It is also possible to make an even shorter circuit of 3 miles by starting from Skeffington and turning back through Welsh Myers before reaching Skeffington wood at the foot of the hill.

From the Rose and Crown in
Tilton walk towards the church and turn right along Main Street. Go through the churchyard gate on your left and walk along the churchyard path towards the church, passing it on your left and rejoining Main street by the old school. (This route cuts out a bit of road walking and takes you through the pretty churchyard.)
Fork left along Loddington Road and in 300 yards turn right and take the gravel drive to Shepherds Cottage (now being restored to a state no shepherd would have recognised). The bridleway leaves the track at the end of the first field and goes diagonally left down to the corner of the field, where it rejoins the drive to cross the stream. Continue close to the stream on your right, leaving Shepherds Cottage up on your left. Walking with the stream on your right cross through the line of hawthorn trees ahead (there is a little bridle gate half hidden in the hedge) and continue through two more fields with bridle gates in quick succession.
Veer left uphill to skirt a fir plantation. From the corner of the plantation the line of the path goes to a large isolated tree beyond which is a cart bridge over the stream. (If there is a good headland on your right, it may prove more

pleasant to walk beside the stream until you meet this cart bridge which is about 200 yards left of the corner of the field; but you need to keep your eyes open for the bridge when the undergrowth is high! You might miss it!)

Cross the cartbridge and go into a vast undulating field. Make for the corner of the field which juts out to your left. Here you meet the Eyebrook stream on your left. Negotiating the rest of this path is difficult because it has for years been obstructed by crops and not reinstated by the farmer, although it is a popular route with walkers. Some people try struggling through the crops along the correct route which goes along high ground above the stream. To do this you need to keep parallel with pylon lines away to the right, or set your sights on Welsh Myers farm on the skyline, walking approximately parallel with the stream below you on your left until you cross Skeffington Wood Lane and continue in the same direction to reach the gate on the top of the hill beyond the lane.

Some people choose to avoid the ploughed land and take the easier route by walking along the Eyebrook edge of the field, keeping close to the stream until they meet Skeffington Wood Lane. But there is no proper headland beside the stream and there is the difficulty of crossing a feeder stream.

If you choose to follow the stream because the crops are high you can cross this feeder stream by turning right to reach the cart bridge (at the end of the hedge). This bridge is on the true line of the path. If you return to the stream, you can follow it to the lane.

If you intend shortening the walk and omitting the circuit to Skeffington you can turn left when you reach the lane and walk through the wood. OMIT THE FOLLOWING PAGES OF INSTRUCTIONS FOR THE ROUTE TO SKEFFINGTON. CONTINUE FROM PAGE 38 col. 3.

To continue to Skeffington *(via Welsh Myers)*
If you have walked beside the

stream you need to turn right when you reach the lane and walk uphill for 200 yards and then turn left to regain the line of the path to Welsh Myers and Skeffington Lodge.

Go uphill in the field beyond Skeffington Wood Lane to reach the gate on the top of the hill.

From the gate at the top of the hill you can clearly see your next goal. The houses on the hill ahead of you are Welsh Myers and Skeffington Lodge farm. Continue in the same direction over the brow of the hill passing close to the corner of a field which juts out on your left and continue downhill to cross the hedge on your left about 50 yards above the stream.

Cross the brick cart bridge and go uphill moving away from the hedge on your right, to a gate on the horizon. Follow the hedge on your right and walk uphill past Welsh Myers farm, keeping in the same direction until you meet Skeffington Lodge farm drive.

Turn right and follow the drive until it takes a sharp bend left. Keep straight on, going through the farm gate and walking diagonally across two fields to meet the main A47 Uppingham Road at a footpath sign. You need to keep in a straight line across fields on the other side of the main road to reach Skeffington. The footpath sign on the other side of the road is, however, a little to your left, so you need to go back on yourself for a hundred yards and then resume the direction you need.

Make for the left side of a red brick barn in the corner of the field. The path continues straight ahead. Go to the left side of the house in front of you. (An old stile leads you into the garden of this house, and the OS Pathfinder map shows the path as going along the right hand side of the garden and through the narrow gap between house and hedge. The owners have, however, constructed an unofficial diversion to the left of the house, where they have planted beech and conifer hedges to mark the path onto the road. This is now the only way you can avoid the dangerous barbed wire obstructions. The path needs to be legalised, waymarked and signposted on the road. It is a very pleasant alternative.)

Turn right along the road and join the main village street in Skeffington. (The church and the lovely Skeffington Hall are along the road to your left.) To reach the main A47 road walk slightly uphill from this junction to pass the Fox and Hounds pub on your right.

From Skeffington

With the Fox and Hounds pub on your right, cross the A47 at the junction with Skeffington Lane and follow the signposted Field Road ahead. This is a lovely curving track, descending to cross the stream and rising again to give magnificent views.

Go over the crest of the hill, passing one hedge on your left and follow the lane downhill, passing one gateway on your right.

IF YOU ARE TAKING THE SHORT 3 MILE CIRCUIT, STARTING FROM SKEFFINGTON, you need to turn right at the next gate and follow the route TO SKEFFINGTON via Welsh Myers described on page 37 col. 3.

To return to Tilton, via Skeffington Wood Lane, continue downhill and go through Skeffington Wood, taking the left fork as you enter it. *The wood is a joy at all seasons, and the lane, although open to traffic, has hedgerows which are in spring full of red campions, forget me nots and violets.*

Pass Wood Farm. At the top of the hill you reach Tilton wood (full of bluebells and campions and other wild flowers in season and alive with birdsong) on your right and open views over old gravel pits to your left.

At the T-junction turn left for 300 yards until you reach Tilton Grange farm. Turn right and go between the stone farm buildings and follow the track along the hedge on your left. Keep this hedge on your left and walk along the bridleway towards the lovely hill of Colborough, surmounted by trees.

(Here you really feel you are on an old straight track, passing close to the ancient hill site and making towards Whatborough Hill the ancient British Hill Fort site.)

Keep close to the hedge on your left

Walk 5 – Tilton

and pass Colborough Hill on your right. In the next field Tennis Wood is some way away to your left. Keep parallel with it and continue in the same direction for three fields, walking with the hedge close to your right in the last field and emerging on the main Oakham road by the Tilton railway bridge and station cottages.(The Salisbury Arms pub is to your left along the road.)

If you stand on the bridge, beware of the traffic. Below you on one side of the line is the NATURE RESERVE and the other a private house and poultry sheds where the station buildings stood. Beside the railway bridge is a little bridle gate which used to lead down to the railway line and the crossing over the lines to the continuation of our path which goes steeply uphill on the far side of the track to cross one field, and meet the Hyde Lodge road just to the south of White Lodge Farm. This path is however under dispute at the moment so it is perhaps easier to turn right over the bridge and risk life and limb by walking along the main Oakham road for 300 yards.

Turn right along the road for 300 yards and then take the road on your left. Walk along this delightful quiet lane, passing White Lodge farm and the interesting remains of ironstone quarrying on your left.
The lane forks left to Stone Lodge farm and you have a choice of routes. Continue on the right hand fork to the top of the hill to see the view and swing back on yourself to cross down the field to meet the left hand fork of the track: or take the short cut along the left fork until you reach a horse trough crossing on your left about 200 yards before Stone Lodge farm.
Go over the stone horse trough crossing and walk with the fence on your left, making straight for Tilton Church spire on the horizon.
Halstead Farm, your next goal, is on a promontory just to the left of the church spire. Take note of this direction, because as you descend to cross the railway line you lose sight of the landmarks and you have to go uphill across a huge, featureless ploughed field.
A stile takes you over the wire fence

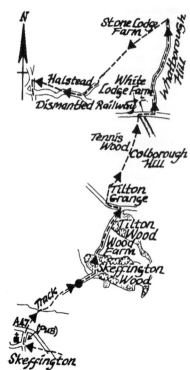

on your left and down to a second stile which leads you across the old railway line. Keep in the right direction and you should reach the hedge ahead of you at a gap where a corner juts out. Walk with the hedge on your left (the waymarking incorrectly indicates a route to the left of the hedge) and meet the lane to Halstead farmhouse (where one can purchase delicious teas and farm produce).

Walk uphill along the farm drive with its newly planted chestnut avenue to meet the main road. Turn right and walk through Halstead village. Halfway down the hill, before the bend in the road, a footpath sign on your right enables you to keep straight on, walking close to a hedge on your left, to meet the Marefield lane at the left of Tilton School grounds.

Turn left to reach Tilton church and the centre of the village.

Walk 5 – Tilton

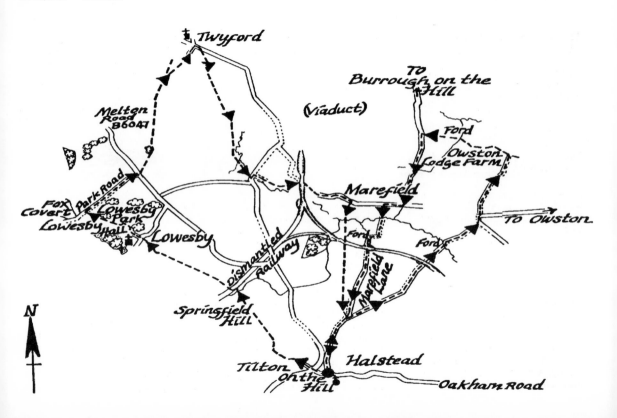

Walk 6 – Tilton

TILTON · MAREFIELD · TILTON

A short 4 $\frac{1}{2}$ mile stroll along good ancient tracks and quiet lanes through one of the hilly parts of Leicestershire. There are lovely views over rolling farmland hills and the surrounding villages and hamlets.
The walk can be extended by adding on the walk from Tilton to Lowesby.

From Tilton with your back to the church and the Rose and Crown walk towards the Melton Road and Marefield Lane, passing close to the public telephone box.
Take the right fork, a No Through Road, and walk along Marefield Lane, past the village school. Pass the de-restriction sign and admire the views straight ahead over Marefield towards Somerby and Burrough on the Hill.
At the Y junction of lanes take the right fork and walk past Red Lodge Farm (where the path becomes a bit muddy). Continue along the green track, crossing the old railway

bridge (East Norton to John O' Gaunt and Melton) and walking with the hedge on your right to join the green lane which descends to the ford.
Cross this as best you can and walk uphill with the hedge on your left through two fields to the top of the hill where you meet the road at a junction.
Take the road signposted to Owston. After 100 yards when the road bends sharp right, keep straight on along the old county road to Newbold, 1 mile away. (We are not going as far as Newbold and need to turn left after half a mile, before we reach the stream.)
In the third field turn left through a gate into a field with a hedge about 50 yards to your right. The path meets this hedge and crosses through it and then follows the farm track which leads to Owston Lodge, keeping this hedge on your left until you meet the stream.
Here you need to turn right and go through the bridle gate so that you pass to the right of the farm.

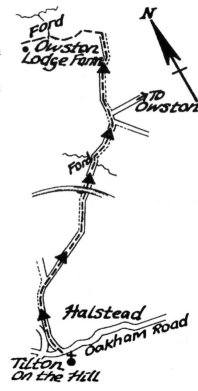

Walk 6 – Tilton

Cross diagonally over this small field to a stile between a tree and a telegraph pole and enter the second field close to a hedge on your right. Follow this hedge all the way to the road.

The house on the road is White House Farm and if you were continuing to Twyford you would continue in the same direction, passing this house on your right and crossing the site of the lost village of North Marefield.

To return to Tilton *via Marefield* turn left and walk along the road for three quarters of a mile. As you go downhill you can see Tilton church spire peeping over the hill and you can pick out the track which you are going to take to reach it.
At the T-junction turn right. The hamlet of Marefield is ahead of you. The lane to Tilton is on your left before you reach the village and will lead you back across lovely rolling countryside, over the dismantled railway line, to the Y-junction where we started.
Tilton village lies half a mile ahead.

Half a mile beyond Tilton lies Halstead, (where the farm of Halstead House serves lovely teas and snacks). Have you walked far enough to deserve a treat?

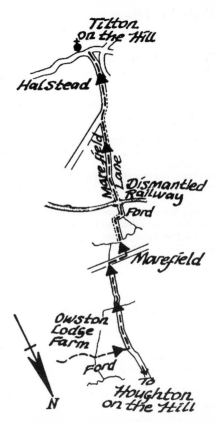

Walk 7 – Tilton

TILTON · LOWESBY
MAREFIELD · TWYFORD ·
TILTON ·
$7\frac{1}{2}$ miles

A delightful circuit through a spectacularly lovely hilly area, from the high ground of Tilton on the Hill, through the beautiful parkland of Lowesby, north to Twyford and back through the little hamlet of Marefield.

The first part of the walk is through pasture valleys. The Twyford part is ploughed and you may experience some difficulty with unmarked paths. If crops obstruct your way it is best to walk single file keeping in the right direction unless a very good headland path has been left. If you do walk round the edge of a field, make sure you take note of your exit point, so that you can regain the right path. (And report any difficulties to the Footpath Officer, County Hall.)

The footpath from Marefield to Tilton is neglected because it has been obstructed for so long and because walkers have taken the easy way out and walked the lane which we used in the Tilton-Marefield walk. But, with perseverance, your feet may help restore this to a well trodden path!

From Tilton church pass the Rose and Crown on your left and walk along Leicester Road. At the T-junction with the main Melton Road (B 6047) cross through the gap on the other side of the road (towards some bungalows) and turn left along the service road for a few yards.

Turn right along Digby Close and find the space between houses Numbered 16 and 17. Go through the farm gate at the end of this little lane. There is a footpath sign to Lowesby and spectacular views down the valley.

Walk downhill parallel with a hedge on your left and swing left to meet the bottom corner of the field. Go through the bridle gate and walk through the little hedged corridor to the pair of farm gates ahead. Go through the left gate and walk with the hedge on your right

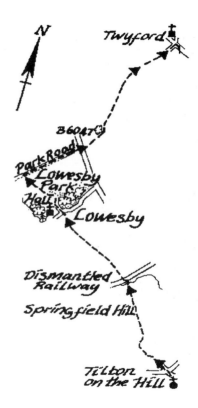

for a short distance (about 100 yards) and then cross through the gate into the field on your right. Continue in the same direction, moving gradually away from the hedge which is now on your left and swinging right before you reach the bottom of the field.

Your route is now along the valley, keeping along the same contour, about half way up the hill, keeping parallel with the stream on your left. (Do not climb up the hill on your right but keep at this level across the long field.) The track is usually visible on the ground.

Cross through a farm gate half way up the hedge ahead of you and walk with the fence (and footings of an old stone wall) on your left.

Pass close to Springfield Farm on your left.

(The D4 path here swings off to your right. This makes a lovely picnic spot by the wood, but it is not the route we're taking!)

Follow the farm track downhill to cross the stream. When the track swings right you need to go straight ahead to cross the dismantled railway line. (You are making for the large pylon at the other side of the line.)

Climb the railway crossing steps by the footpath sign and descend a sloping track down to the line, where you need to pick your way across the old railway station and goods yard, walking under the power lines to reach the hand gate at the top of the opposite embankment, emerging near the pylon.

Walk uphill away from the hedge on your right to meet a hedge junction where you continue uphill close to the hedge on your right. Cross the fence at the top of the field.

This leads you into a corner of the next field, where you continue with the hedge close to your right for a few yards. When the hedge ends continue in the same direction along the top of the hill. Lowesby church tower will miraculously appear straight ahead of you!

(The views here, as elsewhere on this walk, are very beautiful.)

When you meet the far hedge cross the fence at a waymark sign (just to the left of a new plantation of fir trees) and then turn right to walk with the hedge on your right for two fields, heading straight for Lowesby church and emerging on the road opposite the old village school.

(There is a telephone box here but the village affords few other facilities).

A small detour through the churchyard makes a pleasant route (though we are going to rejoin the road to Lowesby Hall which lies straight ahead of us). Turn left to walk through the churchyard. Pass the church on your right and walk towards the lovely Lowesby Hall (gardens occasionally open to the public). Turn right before you reach the Hall gate and walk with the hedge on your left.

From the road which leads into Lowesby Hall we now need to make a semi-circular sweep round the house. Cross the road which goes to the hall and go through the bridle gate opposite you. Turn left and walk parallel with the hall fence and ha ha wall until you meet the avenue of trees which leads from the hall gates.

The grassy track through this avenue of trees may not be a public right of

Walk 7 – Tilton

way so it may be advisable to walk along the footpath which goes beside it, to meet Park Road.

Cross the avenue of trees and walk slightly away from it. You are making for the right of Fox Covert which is ahead of you beyond Park road (which can just be seen between the two bits of woodland to your left). You should emerge on the Lowesby Park road at a footpath sign about 200 yards above the brook and Fox Covert.

Turn right and walk uphill along the Park road. This takes you over the brow of the hill and down to the B6047 Melton road.

Cross the road and go through the gates opposite. Keep in the same direction. Pass a triangular spinney on your left and walk on to pass a second triangular spinney in the next field.

Here you need to cross the way-marked fence on your left and continue in the same direction but with the hedge on your right.

You need to go up the far left corner of the field ahead and the easiest way to get there is to walk with the hedge

on your right until you meet the farm track and then turn left along the track until you meet the clump of trees just before the farm. (The path should cross the fields diagonally but the crossings are obstructed.)

Turn right and walk with the hedge on your left along a good track (paved at the moment with old gym shoes and rubber boots!)
(We are now walking practically due north to Twyford. The impressive viaduct near Marefield can be seen to our right.)

Go through the corner of the field and walk with the hedge on your right. Cross under the pylon lines. When the hedge bends right continue straight ahead, cutting across the corner of the field to reach the farm gate straight ahead. You now make for Twyford village, which can be seen ahead. At the end of the field you will be walking with a stream in the valley on your left.

Your next crossing is about 200 yards to the right of it. In the next field move slightly right uphill to

leave the stream. Make for the right of Twyford village ahead of you. There is crossing hidden in the far right corner of the field, beyond a steep little slope (and a plank to take you over the quagmire!).

The stile here brings you out into the corner of a field with a hedge on your left. Go up the bank and pass the little playing area on your right. Walk along Loseby Lane to meet the Burrough Road near the centre of Twyford opposite the old village school.

(Twyford pub and church are to your left. The pub serves meals. Our route continues to the right.)

From Twyford to Tilton via Marefield, walk along Burrough road for 100 yards. At the derestriction sign turn right and follow the footpath sign, to walk with the stream on your left.

Keep to the higher ground away from the stream (to avoid the wet area) and make towards the brick barn ahead of you, slightly to your right. The waymarked stile is just to the left of the barn, beside a tree.

Cross the stile and turn right along the farm track. Walk uphill to pass to the left of the barn.

The next field is a very large one and you need to cross it diagonally, moving uphill with nothing much to guide you until you can see the spire of Tilton church ahead. Keep parallel with the pylon lines which are way over to your right and make your way (through the crops if necessary) to the far left corner of the field.

There is a wide gap in the corner of the field, where a hedge has been removed, and a wide gateway in the hedge ahead of you to your left.

As you go through this gap you can see The Dairy Farm at the far side of the field. You now need to turn right, to walk with the hedge on your right to reach a farm bridge in the corner of the field. (The map indicates that you should cross the hedge half way down the hedge but there is no easy way through and this is the route the farmer expects you to use.)

Once across the farm bridge go diagonally left to walk uphill over the brow of the next field, still making for Tilton church spire which is just a needle point on the highest hill, between trees.

Go down to the corner of the field where a corner of hedge juts out. The easiest crossing point is just to the right of this corner, where there is a ricketty old gate, festooned in barbed wire. (The whole of this path needs properly clearing and waymarking!)

In the next field continue in the same direction to the bottom corner of the field. Here you need to cross the stream junction, negotiating your way across the first stream and then walking with the second one on your left until you reach the lane, by the footpath sign.

Here there is a big green verge. Turn left for a short distance and then turn right for a quarter of a mile along the lovely lane to Marefield, following the stream on your right.

Go under the railway line, and continue into the village of Marefield. You need to turn right and walk due south from Marefield into Tilton. The start of the path is rather tricky but the way is so lovely that it is worth persevering.

The footpath sign points you to the

garden door of The Chase, (opposite the donkey stud farm). If you are worried by this seeming intrusion, you could knock on the house door to inform the owners that you are about to walk the footpath! (I have always found them most helpful. It is an acknowledged right of way and the owners are aware of it.)

Go through the garden door and walk along the path beside the house and down the garden path to a bridle gate. (The published line goes across two gardens but this route saves embarrassment.)

Cross the farm track, pass the stable shed and swing right to cross the farm gate. Turn left and walk down the field close to the hedge on your left.

Cross the cart bridge over the stream and walk straight uphill to reach a ladder-crossing over the old railway line. Keep in the same direction and descend the other side.

Keep making for the spire of Tilton. Cross a dip and make for the left side of a clump of trees on the hill in front of you. (These fields are usually ploughed and if the going gets tough you can join the lane which is now close to your left.) If you keep straight for Tilton spire you will emerge at the lane junctions by the footpath sign. Walk up the lane (you know now why the village's full title is Tilton ON THE HILL). Turn round for a lingering look back. A whole panorama is there spread out. Burrough Hill, Burrough on the Hill, Somerby, Waltham mast, Ratcliffe on Soar power station and the Charnwood hills can all be seen on a clear day.

Pass the school and arrive at Tilton church and Pub.

D

Rolleston

Billesdon 9 miles east of Leicester at the foot of the marlestone edge, where we enter the belt of stone buildings. The village stands in a sheltered site settled by the Anglo Saxons. (A magnificent Anglo Saxon brooch was found here dating from about 550 A.D.) The settlement was called Bil's dun (hill pasture), because of its proximity to the Coplow hill which must have been a primitive landmark. The name Coplow suggests a burial mound: Cop (top) hlaw (hill, especially a burial mound). The hill has a very distinctive silhouette made by a clearing in the wood.

Billesdon was in 1066 part of an estate which included Rolleston, Goadby, Keythorpe and Hallaton and belonged to Tochi, a Danish settler who gave his name to Tugby and who must have started the building of Tugby church, which has a pre-Norman tower. (Hoskins)

Billesdon Free school was refounded 1650. A plaque on the wall recounts its history. There was an earlier school attended by George Villiers, later Duke of Buckingham, until he was 13, and by George Fox.

Botany Bay fox covert dates from 1790s when the convict settlement was in the news.

Since the by-pass was opened in 1987 Billesdon has become a quiet village. It is possible to park on the village square. There is also a little space near the church.

Cold Newton a very interesting little deserted village. It isn't actually on our route, but only requires a short detour to visit it. The main street, now a sunken hollow way, still forms the footpath through the site. And remains of an old stone wall can be seen.

Rolleston The Tudor hall and its 13th century towered church (rebuilt 1740) nestle behind a high wall. Firth tells us that it was famous as a hunting seat, once lived in by a master of the Quorn and later by Oswald Mosley and by Viscount Churchill, who in 1899 restored the little church. The house has a wonderful yew hedge 20' high . The church yard has a slender cross among the trees. The lovely fish pond is regularly fished. The stables have recently been done up as a housing complex of desirable residences, so perhaps the old comment about there being more horses than people at Rolleston will no longer be true.

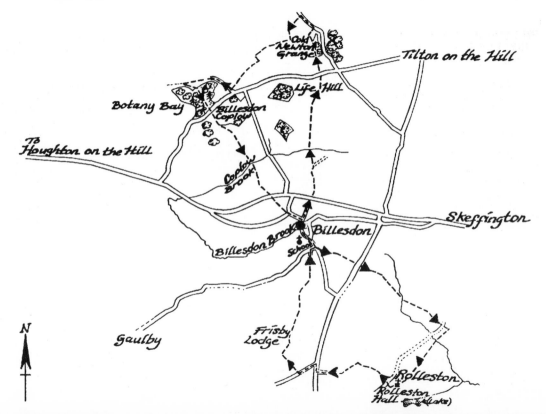

BILLESDON · COLD NEWTON · BOTANY BAY · BILLESDON · 6 miles

A moderately strenuous 6 miles along straight and ancient pathways. Many of the paths are now ploughed and the ground is hilly. This makes the walking a bit tough occasionally, but the views are correspondingly delightful. The views from Sludge Hall hill are dramatic. The woodland and valleys are beautiful at all seasons. The route described through Botany Bay Covert is slightly longer than the direct road route, but is worth the detour for the joys of walking through woodland. It is possible to walk along the road to Cold Newton, with its medieval village site, which lies on the northern edge of the present village. This adds on half a mile each way. *Billesdon lies 9 miles west of Leicester on the road to Uppingham. It is possible to park near the church or in the Market Place on Leicester Road, where buses stop en route between Uppingham and Leicester.*

From Billesdon Market Place, at the junction of Church street and Leicester Road, cross the main road and walk up Long Lane. At the end of the lane go through the farm gate and walk uphill with the hedge on your right. Make your way slightly left (Billesdon Coplow is straight ahead of you) to find the new stile in the dip of the field. This takes you across the new Billesdon By-pass road to a stile opposite.

Turn right and walk up the gravel track parallel with the road (on your right) to cross the stile by the gate at the top. Turn left and walk along the old footpath, with the hedge on your left. (Billesdon church spire is behind you and Billesdon Coplow slightly to your left.)

Follow the hedge on your left as it crosses the brow of the hill, passing a small reservoir over to your right. Go through the gate in the wire fence. Here you need to move diagonally right and go downhill, making for the far right corner of the field below you. (You can walk for a short distance down a sunken grassy track but make sure you do not go too far along it. You need to cross into the field on your left so that you can keep in the northerly direction you have already walked from Billesdon. The path is not waymarked and the crossings are not good in the first two hedges.)

From the corner of the field cut across the little corner of the next field and cross the stream (there is a concrete cart bridge to your left). Go through the gate at the far side of the stream and continue in the same direction up the next, big (ploughed) field. The hedge and a red brick barn are some way to your right. Go up to the gate in the far right corner of the field.

From this gate, continue northwards. (Please note that the walkable route is not quite as shown on definitive maps.) Walk for a short distance with a hedge on your right. When it ends continue across the dip in the field. Go uphill past isolated trees on your left, keeping parallel with a wire fence on your right and a long ridge of hill beyond it.

Aim for the gate on the skyline. (The crossing should be to the left of this gate but it is obstructed at present.)

At the top of the hill the land to the right of the gate is pitted with old gravel workings, which are now interesting humps and hollows where sheep browse. Nether Court farm is in the far corner of this field. Go through the gate and walk with the hedge on your right. The hill ahead is Life Hill. Many hedges have been removed but if you continue north and keep the hedge on your right about 100 yards away from you, until you see the trees lining Tilton Lane, you should reach a footpath sign near a gate on the road.

(The true crossing is slightly left of the gate, opposite the footpath sign on the other side of the road.) Cross the road and go through the wrought iron gates into the field opposite. (This is the camp site for Guides and you pass their camp hut on your right.) Go to the far right corner of the field, where you should find a stile in the spinney.

Cross through the spinney and turn left to continue in the same direction, passing through a line of isolated trees.

This is a marvellous viewing point. Lowesby Hall and Twyford are ahead of you and below you is Sludge Hall farm riding stables. Continue along the ridge. When it swings right make your way down the steep hill keeping the wood on your left. Pass close to Sludge Hall (an impressive white building nestling in trees) on your left. Go through a little white handgate, cross the drive and go through the second gate opposite you. Turn right and walk close to the drive on your right. Go through the gate in the hedge ahead and turn left along the road to Cold Newton.

At the end of the first field (before you reach the old railway line) turn left. *(You are now in Quenby Hall grounds with their distinctive white topped red gates. You can see the Hall over to your right as you walk along the farm drive.)* As you approach Cold Newton Grange the drive swings left. The

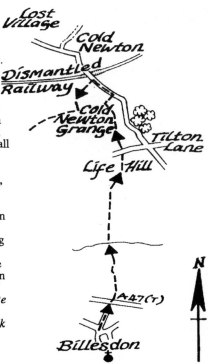

true line of the path follows it and swings right just before the house, going through a farm gate and then crossing to the far right corner of the field where a gap in the hedge on your right takes you through the hedge. A left turn here brings you out in line with Cold Newton Lodge, following the hedge on your left. (Many walkers avoid this 'left and right' detour to the Grange and continue straight ahead, following the hedge on their left all the way to Cold Newton Lodge, the next farmhouse. There is usually quite a good track to follow.)

Go through the double farm gates and pass Cold Newton Lodge on your left. Turn left, following the hedge, and cross the waymarked fence in the corner of the field. Turn right to walk along the farm drive until you meet the road.

You are now going to walk through Botany Bay wood, which is a good way of avoiding the busy Billesdon-Tilton road. Turn right and walk along the Hungarton road for 300 yards, passing the tip of Botany Bay Wood.

Turn left through the open gateway and walk along the old county road. At the end of the field you need to swing back on yourself to reach the main track through Botany Bay wood. (If you walk close to the hedge and wood on your right you will reach the gate into the wood.) *The route through the wood is straight and easy to follow. It has recently been surfaced in places with gravel. The wood is full of birdsong and alive with rabbits and the track makes a pleasant alternative to the busy Tilton road.*

Turn right for a short distance along the road and turn left to the post box and footpath sign. Walk through the impressive gateway of Billesdon Coplow and along the drive, towards the stables. (The house stands on the hill to your left).

Go to the right of the stables and continue in the same direction, passing Inkpot Cottage on your right. A gate between hedges takes you into a field with the hedge on your left. Go to the right of the stable shed ahead of you and cross the plank and stile.

Note Billesdon church spire ahead of you on the skyline. You now aim directly towards it, but it will disappear from view. Go diagonally across a large, oddly shaped field. (At the end of the field there is a long narrow "corridor" leading to large farm barns and a silo on your left.) You need to cross the hedge ahead of you. (A waymark sign would be useful here!) In the next field you should have a curving hedge and a stream on your left. Cross the cartbridge half way along this hedge and walk in the same direction with the hedge now on your right.

You now keep in this direction over mainly pasture fields all the way to Billesdon. The first field has a fence crossing and barbed wire, the second has a substantial footbridge 40 yards from the hedge on the right. In the third field you walk along a ridge in a ridge-and-furrow field. Make for houses on the skyline. Pass to the right of a barn and go through a stiled wire fence and a hedge fence.

You are now approaching the new by-pass road. Go to the right hand corner of this field. A trio of stiles (with no connecting plank) leads you to the embankment of the new road. Cross the road and the stile opposite.

In the next big field you need to walk uphill to meet the hedge on your left, aiming for the right of the roof of the bungalow which peeps over the hill. You now have Billesdon Church steeple magnificently ahead of you. Walk with the hedge on your left to pass the bungalow and cross the stile in the far left corner of the field, which leads into a little path between houses. Meet the road and turn right to the road junction. Turn left to reach Billesdon Market Place at the junction of Leicester Road and Church street.

Walk 9 – Billesdon

BILLESDON • SKEFFINGTON VALE FARM • ROLLESTON • ASHLANDS • BILLESDON • 5 miles

From Billesdon church walk uphill along Church Road passing the old school on your right. Pass the road junction to Gaulby and Frisby on your right and continue uphill until the road swings right. Leave the road and continue straight ahead, going through the gate on the left hand side of the road.

Walk uphill to cross this field diagonally. (This is Kates Hill. There is a mound over to your left.) Descend to a gate about 100 yards from the bottom left corner. Go uphill in the next field parallel with the hedge on your left. (There are fine views from the top.) Continue downhill to meet the road at a footpath sign. (The fence crossing is rather rough and there is a ditch.)

Cross the road and negotiate the next rough crossing. The field has a corner which drops down to the right. Keep to the high ground and

make for the left hand corner of the hedge in front of you. (Ignore the gate which is directly in front of you.)

Walk with the hedge on your right. Cross into the next field by using the gate ahead slightly to your left. From the gate make your way gradually back to the hedge on your right, passing the corner where the hedge turns away. Continue downhill in the same direction to reach the bottom corner near some trees. Go through the bridle gate and cross the cartbridge over the stream. Turn right and cross the concrete plank bridge in the corner of the field. Clamber up the steep bank and continue uphill in the next field. Continue in the same direction to meet the hedge on your right. (This is a very long narrow field and it is usually ploughed. If the way is obstructed by crops you can move to your right and follow the headland on your right.) When you reach the gap in the hedge, just before it makes a little kink, turn right and then left

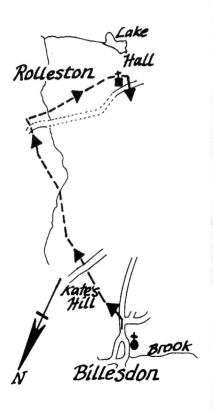

immediately, to continue in the same general direction. The hedge is now on your left. Move to your right to cut off a little corner of this field. Skeffington Vale farmhouse is in the trees ahead of you. In the next field walk away from the hedge on your left to meet the gate beside the footpath sign. This brings you out on the lane, opposite the drive to the house.

It is possible to turn right here and walk along the lane to reach the Rolleston crossroads, but it is more of an achievement to use the footpath.

Go up the drive towards the house and turn right just before you reach it. Walk parallel with the hedge on your left and pass the beautiful house and the thatched cottage beyond it. Go downhill to cross the stream by a good footbridge just to the right of the circular fenced paddock and a telegraph pole. Climb the rough bank of the next field and pass three isolated trees on your left. Use this line of three trees as a marker to point your way up this very long (ploughed) field. If

you keep just left of the crest of the hill you can keep roughly parallel to the hedge on your left and eventually make for Rolleston church tower, in the dark trees on the skyline. You should reach the end of the field just to the left of an old quarry (now being filled in). (If the way is obstructed by barbed wire you can move right to cross through a gate and then turn left to cross the fence into the quarry field.) Continue in the same direction to reach the lane by Rolleston church. There is a footpath sign in the bottom right hand corner of the field.

(If you wish to see the lake you need to turn left at this point and then return to continue the walk.)

Turn right and walk along the lane, passing the church in private grounds on your left.

Follow the lane round to the junction of gated roads (to New Inn, Three Gates, Skeffington and Billesdon.)

Take the track to Billesdon and go downhill to the gate (as in the Rolleston-Ashlands walk). In the

next field, leave the track and walk close to the hedge on your left. In the far left corner turn left through the gate and walk with the hedge on your right.

Go through the gate and turn right in the next field to walk up towards an imposing red brick house with stables. Follow the drive past the house to reach the main road.

Turn right along this road and then turn left along the gated road to Illston. Walk with Long Plantation on your left. (The big house ahead of you is Ashlands, but we are not going that far. We are going to leave the road and turn right to return to Billesdon.)

The route now is mainly arable and can be hard going for the next three fields, although the route is waymarked.

When you reach the second field on your right, turn right and walk along the headland with the hedge on your right. Go down a slight dip and up the other side for about 200 yards. Turn right through a gateway and cross the next field.

Ahead of you there is to your left a small red brick ruin. Your waymarked crossing is to the right of it, in line with Billesdon church spire.

Aim for the church spire and go uphill to the gap in the next hedge. In the third field continue on the high ground (the spire is now a little to your left) making for a bridlegate which is to the left of two trees. This brings you out into the corner of a pasture field. Walk with the hedge on your right.

When the hedge makes a slight bend right, keep in the same direction. (Ignore the waymarked path on your left.) Go through the gate in the middle of the hedge ahead.

Walk with the hedge on your left. Go over the rough stream bed crossing and continue to the field gate, passing large storage sheds on your right.

Move right to cut across the field to a fence crossing (about 100 yards from the storage sheds) which leads you into a small triangular field at the foot of some houses. Turn left to reach a second rough stile which leads onto a grassy track at the bottom of the gardens of the houses. This track leads you between fencing

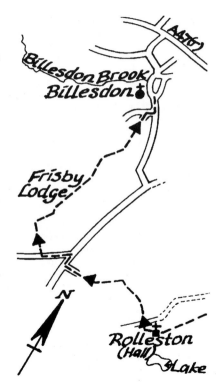

to reach Glebe Close and Vicarage Close. The church spire can be seen rising rather incongruously above a bungalow ahead of you. Turn right along the Frisby road and left along Church road to reach the church and the centre of Billesdon.

Burton Overy

Burton Overy lies just east of Great Glen on the A6 between Leicester and Market Harborough. To the west of the village are earthworks known as "The Banks" on each side of the stream. It has been suggested that this may be the remains of the deserted medieval village of Novery or the moated site of Noverey Manor. In the 1285 Charter Rolls the village name is Burton Novery.

The Church of St Andrew is early 14th century and very fine, though it seems hardly appropriate to describe its extensive reconstruction as 'Perpendicular' when you look at the two wings which seem to lean away from one another!

There are several 17th century timber framed buildings. One of these, South View, has mud walls and a brick gable-end dated 1739. Manor house farm in Back Lane has a moulded beam dated FRA (Robert and Anne Freeman?) 1650 WM6. There is an imposing rectory built c.1700-1710 and several houses with good Georgian brick fronts. The Old Manor House was probably built by John Nedham, gent., who bought the manor in 1618.

Carlton Curlieu lies 9 miles SE of Leicester above the 450 feet contour. It is bounded on the north by the Gartree road and on the west by one of the head-streams of the River Sence which separates it from the village of Burton Overy. The village consists of a few farm-houses and cottages grouped near the church and the rectory. Most of the houses were built of red brick in the early 19th century.

The manor of Carlton Curlieu belonged to the Priory of Ulverscroft. The site of the medieval manor house is marked by the moat beside the road just to the south of the T-junction.

Carlton Curlieu was the centre of one of the bailiwicks of the honor of Leicester. It seems probable that Carlton Curlieu became so known as a result of the connexion with the Curly family. It is written as Carleton Curly in the 1217 Close Rolls. William Curly died in 1253.

The manor was bought by the Bales of Saddington, who built the present Carlton Curlieu Hall about 1630. The Hall stands in its own grounds to the SE of the church. An ironstone gable-end overlooking the yard has a date tablet of 1636 with initials I.O and T.O. Sir John Bale was made High Sheriff of Leicester in 1624. He became a "great sufferer in the Royalist cause" and his house was garrisoned by troops in the Civil War. He was committed to the Tower when the Royal cause failed in 1655, accused of plotting against Cromwell. He was later rewarded for his support by Charles II.

The church (of St Mary the Virgin) has a Norman arch and it is recorded that there was a Priest here in 1086. Only the lower stages of the 12th-century tower remain. In the church is a monument to Sir John Bale, who died in 1621 and his wife Frances, who died in 1624. There are also tablets to the Palmer family 1840-1905.

The origin of the place name is Scandinavian, probably meaning 'Freepeople's town'. The historian Burton, writing in 1620, notes the peculiar manner of speech of the inhabitants. He writes that "all those who are born here have an harsh and rattling kind of speech, uttering their words with great difficulty, and wharling in the throat, and cannot well pronounce the letter R." Fuller, later in the 17th century attributed this "to some occult quality in the elements of the place" but it was more probably due to the fact that in origin Carlton was a Danish community of free peasants, with their own distinctive speech. By the 18th century this speech was lost and no memory remained of it.

Carlton Clump is a well-known landmark with views right across country to Charnwood Forest.

Illston on the Hill stands on high ground just north of the Roman Gartree road. It consists of one street, a dead end, which was formerly an important packhorse track to the south.

The church of St Michael and All Angels retains some 13th century features. At this time the chapel was shared by Carlton Curlieu and Nosely and the village is still partly in the these two parishes. There are monuments to the Nedham family 1669 1639 1758 etc. in the church.

Illston Grange The house was demolished in 1927, but the impressive red brick clock tower stables remain.

Ashlands on the northern boundary of the parish, is a stone mansion built in 1867 in Tudor style.

Gaulby a tiny village which has had a church since the 12th century. The church was rebuilt in 1520, but only the chancel and the communion rail remain of this building. The present church was built in 1741, financed by William Fortrey, the lord of the manors of Gaulby and Kings Norton. The architect was John Wing, whose son was the architect of the church at Kings Norton. The tall classical towers of both churches are striking.

Gaulby's has distinctive oriental stone pinnacles. (From a distance, from over the fields these have a distinct 'rabbits' ears' appearance!)

A National School was opened in the village in 1875. When Powys-Keck was lord of the manor he built a new school for the children of the neighbouring villages. It was closed in 1950 and the children transferred to Billesdon school.

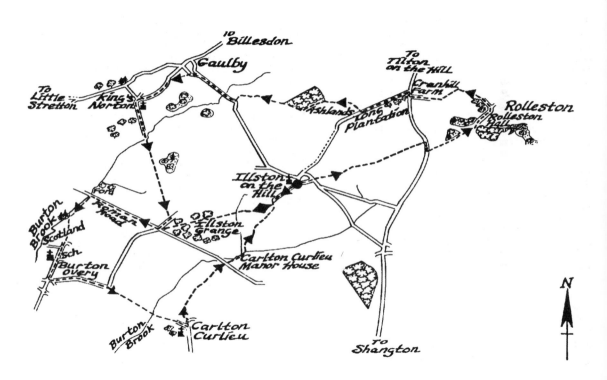

ILLSTON ON THE HILL • BURTON OVERY • CARLTON CURLIEU • ILLSTON ON THE HILL

$5\frac{1}{2}$ miles through gently undulating country. This can be added onto the next walk of $7\frac{1}{2}$ miles to make a good 13 mile figure of eight walk.

From Illston village walk down the main street. Pass the church and the Fox and Goose inn on your right. At the end of the street go through the bridle gate beside the farm gate. (Left of the FP sign.)
Keep close to the hedge on your right, passing the Soar Division Water Works building in the field on your right, and go uphill to the top right corner of the little field. (There is a mound here which looks like an old motte and bailey. It may be a windmill base.)
Go through the handgate and pass a little pond on your right. Keep close to the right hand hedge for two more fields, until you reach the handgate and cartbridge over the stream. You now need to move left of the hedge on your right and aim

straight for Illston Grange stables, with their distinctive red brick tower.
Pass an isolated telegraph pole and go uphill to a gate just to the left of an avenue of trees.
Continue in the same direction (following the power lines) and go through the farm gate. If you keep in the same direction you will come to a gap in the fencing on your left which leads you downhill to join the farm drive and thence to the stable tower. Turn right just here and follow the right fork of the drive.
When it swings left continue straight ahead. Go through the gate into the field opposite. Walk diagonally left across a huge parkland pasture, (passing to the right of a clump of chestnut trees.) Aim for the far corner of the field, where a signpost peeps over the hedge. This indicates the cross roads. (Burton Overy 1 mile Great Glen 3 Kings Norton 1 and the Gartree Road, Unsuitable for Motors.) Cross the double fence to the left of the field corner and turn

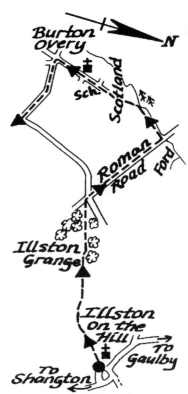

right along the road to meet the cross roads. Go straight ahead along the Gartree Road and walk along the track with the hedge on your right. (Note the fine views of Kings Norton church over to your right.) The track becomes a little lane between hedges and descends to the ford through the stream, where you leave the Roman road.

Cross the stile on your left just before the concrete footbridge and walk with the stream on your right all the way into Burton Overy. (In the second field you need to keep to the high ground and pass to the left of the trees on the bank above the stream. In the third field you need to swing left when you meet the spinney.)

Keep the hedge and stream on your right and walk downhill to cross the cart bridge which is slightly to your left. Go through the gate beyond the cartbridge and walk with the hedge on your left, for two fields. At the left of some ricketty barns a gate leads you into a (muddy) lane. Turn right at the end of the lane and walk into the Scotland area of

Burton Overy. (In 'Scot land' you do not get off scot free of the 'Scot tax.) Swing left at the road junction to reach the church.

Burton Overy church is worth a visit. It has a very interesting collection of memorial slabs, including many to the Coleman family and one to William Knox, elder son of the reverend James Knox, minister of Scone in Scotland, who died in 1817. There are very pretty houses and gardens to be seen in the village. The Bell Inn which used to provide simple refreshment, has recently been re-opened. The post office is the only shop. In the field behind the church are the Banks, ancient earthworks of Novery.

From Burton Overy to Carlton Curlieu

This section of the walk is mainly over green pastures. It begins along a gated road.

From Burton Overy church walk down to the Bell Inn and turn left along the lovely Carlton Lane. There are fine views over open

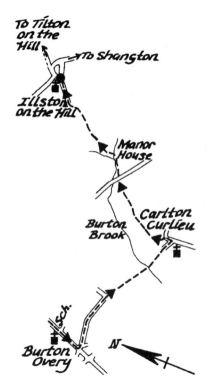

E

ridge and furrow pasture fields. After about half a mile, at the top of the incline, where the road takes a sharp left turn, keep straight on past the farm sheds and go through the right of two farm gates. This leads into the farm yard with the hedge on your left. Go through the gate opposite. Walk downhill with the hedge on your left until you reach the stream. The footbridge is 20 yards to your right.

Make your way up the next field, following the power lines, heading straight for Carlton Curlieu church tower. Go through the farm gate on your left near the top of the hill and turn right to follow the road into the village. Pass the telephone box and the church on your right.

At the T-junction turn left. Walk along the road (to Three Gates) for 100 yards and then turn left at the next junction to follow the bridle road to Illston. This swings right to pass the farm and then continues between hedges for almost a mile. Cross the Gartree Road (metalled at this point) near Carlton Curlieu Manor House farm.

Go through the bridle gate opposite. Keep close to the hedge on your left and pass the farm house on your right. Follow the farm track as it swings left beside the stream. (Ignore stiles or gates on your left. Do not cross the stream yet.) In the corner of the first field go through the double farm gate and cross the cart bridge over the stream. Continue with the hedge on your left to reach the next gate.

The next field is a very large one. It once had a good pack horse track but has been for many years obstructed by crops. This year for the first time the path has been re-instated, so you may be in luck in finding a clearly marked path to take you to Illston.

The path begins 20 yards to the right of the gate and goes straight towards Illston on the Hill church tower. (If it isn't clearly marked, you need to move about 100 yards to your right and then walk parallel with the hedge on your left until you can see Illston church tower.) *(There are lots of interesting fossils and stones in the bare soil of this field.)*

The path brings you out at the far hedge near the little pond where the walk began. Go to the right of the pond, walk through the little bridle gate. Cross the field with the mound in it and go through the gate in the bottom corner by the footpath sign. Walk up the main street of Illston village.

The Fox and Goose pub is an ancient pack horse inn. It wins Best Beer awards and is popular among connoisseurs of good ale. Walkers like the warm welcome they receive. Once refreshed, you might like to add on the following $7\frac{1}{2}$ mile walk to Rolleston.

ILLSTON ON THE HILL • ROLLESTON • ASHLANDS • GAULBY • ILLSTON

7 or 8 miles. A pleasant 3 or 4 hour stroll through mainly pasture land. This is gently rolling country with fine views from the ridges. *Leave Illston village* with the church on your left and pass the telephone box on your right. Take the right fork in the road (opposite the little post box set in the wall of Illston Heights.)
Pass the village hall on your right and emerge on the road opposite the road signs to Gaulby and Kings Norton (1 mile), Three Gates (1 mile) and Goadby (3 miles).
Cross the road and go over the fence opposite. In this big field you have a broken hedge on your right. You need to cut across the corner of the field to cross this hedge through a gap to the left of the one tall tree. Continue in the same direction cutting across the corner of the next field to reach a farm gate which brings you out in the corner of the third field. Continue again in the

same direction, aiming now for a small wood on the hill ahead of you, and cross the stream using the substantial footbridge.
Go uphill to reach the fence at the right of the small wood. Cross the fence and pass Barn farm house on your left. Walk with the hedge on your left for two long fields. At the end of the second field you need to move slightly right to reach the footpath sign on the road just to the right of the big house.
(The signposted route takes you through a little paddock and along the drive of the house but you may prefer to avoid the horses in the paddock and move further to your right to pass the hedge of the paddock on your left. A well used route takes you to the road by a crossing in the corner of the field to the right of the big house and the footpath sign.)
Turn right and walk along the Billesdon-Market Harborough B6047 road for 50 yards and then turn left along the signposted Rolleston road, passing through the lodge gates into the estate lands.

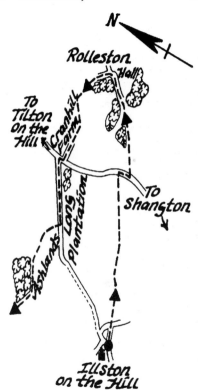

Walk 11 – Illston figure of eight (Burton Overy • Illston • Rolleston)

Ignore the right fork and continue along the horse chestnut drive for three quarters of a mile. Pass the gateway to Rolleston Hall on your right. Cross the cattle grid and pass the large red brick converted stable block on your left.

Turn left at the road junction (towards Billesdon). Ignore the gated road on your right (to Skeffington) and go downhill along the track to Billesdon for 20 yards. Go through the gate at the foot of the dip and swing left, away from the track and follow the hedge on your left.

At the far corner of the field, turn left, go through the gate and walk with the hedge on your right for one field.

Go through the gate and turn right in the next field. Walk uphill to pass Cranhill farm house and stables on your right. The drive leads you back to the Billesdon-Harborough road. Turn right for 50 yards and then left along the road (signposted Gated Road to Illston).

Walk along this road with Long Plantation on your left and fine views on your right, for half a mile. Turn right just before you reach the gated avenue of horse chestnut trees belonging to the big house, Ashlands. (There is a gateway across the road at this point and a waymarked gate on your right). We are going to take the footpath which passes behind the house. Go through the gate and and walk with the hedge of Ashlands on your left, for 20 yards. Turn left through a little handgate and cut across the field to reach the hedge of Ashlands again on your left.

Walk with the hedge on your left and pass the fine house and garden. In the next field follow this hedge downhill to a gate which leads you onto a grassy track between a little wood on your right and a hedge on your left. Go downhill to reach the end of the wood. Go through the gate and turn right, keeping close to the edge of the wood.

You are now heading for Gaulby church tower. Walk with the hedge on your right for three fields, joining a vehicle track, which swings left at the end of the third

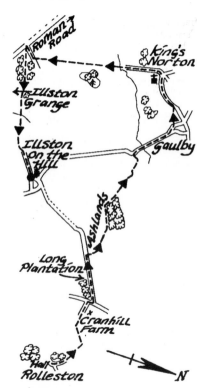

field to meet the Gaulby lane.
Turn right and walk along the road
uphill into GAULBY. Keep on the
left fork, signposted to Kings Norton
and Little Stretton. Pass Wyggeston
farm on your left and turn left
through the next farmyard (Manor
Farm), where there is a convenient
and pleasant short cut to the Kings
Norton lane.
Go through the farmyard to the gate
opposite and continue in the same
direction across one field, aiming
straight for Kings Norton Church
tower. Go through two gates to reach
the lane and continue to walk along it
into the village.

From Kings Norton pass the church
on your left and take the road signposted to Illston. Walk downhill for
a quarter of a mile. At the signpost,
where the road bends left and the
bridle road goes straight on, you have
a choice. You can make a short cut
back to Illston by continuing on this
quiet country road or you can take
the bridle road to Illston Grange,
which adds a mile to the walk.

(Ignore the next paragraph if you
choose the longer route.)

*If you go by road from Kings
Norton to Illston you can take to
the fields again for the last three
fields before Illston church. At the
road junction where you meet the
Illston-Burton Overy road, cross
into the field on your right and
walk straight towards Illston
church tower. (The road on your
left takes a slightly longer route.)
Cross three fields using the church
as your marker. At the top of the
third field pass to the right of a
tree-lined pond. In the next field
cross a stile on your right and then
a fence on your right, into the holly
hedged graveyard of Illston church.
Pass the church on your right to
meet the village street. Turn right
to reach the Fox and Goose pub.*

To Illston via Illston Grange
(This path takes you in a straight
line from Kings Norton to meet the
road near Illston Grange, where you
turn right.) When you reach the
signpost at the bend in the Kings

Norton to Illston road, go through
the gate ahead of you and walk with
the hedge on your right.
Cross the stream and walk uphill
with a fence on your left. Keep the
fence on your left until you have
passed the wood over to your left,
continue in the same direction down
the open field and uphill in the next.
(The track is usually easy to see. It
moves away from the hedge on your
left to meet the tree lined road
across the horizon.)
Turn right and walk along the road
to the road junction. Turn left for a
short distance and then cross the
double fence on your left into
the field.
This is a huge parkland pasture
field. You need to cross it diagonally. Illston Grange is in the far
corner, nestling in trees. You
should reach the grange drive, close
to a clump of horse chestnut trees.
Turn left along the drive. When you
reach the impressive red brick
stables, turn left and walk across the
concrete yard to reach the farm gate.
Go through the gate and swing
right. Cut across the corner of the

field and go through the next farm gate. Continue in the same direction (parallel with the power lines) to cut across the next field to the corner of the field near an avenue of trees. Continue in the same direction, towards Illston church tower, going down the next (ploughed) field. (Keep roughly parallel with the power lines if your way is obstructed by crops.) Cross the cartbridge over the stream near the bottom left corner of the field and go through the little gate. Walk uphill with the hedge on your left for two fields.

At the top of the hill you will pass on your left a little pond. Go through the handgate on your left and walk across the small field with the mound in it. In the bottom right corner go through the gate which leads you into the main street of Illston on the Hill.

The Fox and Goose pub is on your left. You deserve a drink!

Kibworth (from the Anglo Saxon Cybba's worth, Cybba's enclosure. It is recorded in Domesday Book as Chiburde 1125 and later as Kibewrda 1160 Cubworth 1200). Kybeworth Beauchamp is named in 1315 after the Beauchamps, Earls of Warwick. Kibworth Harcourt, a separate manor, was held by the Harcourt family (from Harcourt in Normandy) from 1202 until 1270 when it passed to Walter de Merton and thence to Merton College, Oxford, which he founded. The college still owns much of the land in the area. *The Windmill is a restored Post Mill, with sails.*

Tur Langton *Turling's tun, the village of Turl's people.* The Victorian red brick church, designed by Joseph Goddard, who designed the clock tower and Midland bank in Granby Street, is a replacement for the medieval church whose ruins can still be seen in a field at the other end of the village. It is interesting to see that although the spire is impressive and can be seen from a long distance away, the footpaths naturally converge upon the old church.

The Consecration of the Chapel of Ease is described in the Northampton Mercury Oct 6th 1866: "It is now 15 years since the benefactor of these 5 Parishes conceived his magnificent ideas of beautifying the district in his botanical way.... A few weeks ago the thorough restoration of the church and organ at Church Langton was reported, on Thursday last another instalment of his benefactions was paid. A new church was given to the inhabitants of Tur Langton and a beautiful edifice it is. In the evening the architects and contractors gave a supper to all the workmen that had been employed, at the Bulls Head Inn. Upwards of 30 partook of it. It is doubtful whether Tur Langton will see such another festival for the next century or more to come." (History of the Parish of Langton by John Harwood Hill 1867.)

Church Langton a spectacularly beautiful and impressive church with ancient tombs (and bats) and a list of rectors from 1220, including Polydore Vergil (who wrote a History of England and was a friend of Sir Thomas More) 1503 and William Hanbury 1782 and Thomas Hanbury 1817 and 1848. The old organ originally built in 1759 was used here in the first church performance of Handel's Messiah, at a music festival organised by the famous William Hanbury. The Rev William Hanbury 1725-1778 of Church Langton was an extra-ordinary Georgian rector, philanthropist and eccentric. The living, purchased for him by his father, included the four Langton churches and was one of richest in Leicestershire, in 1750. The young man's interests were throughout his life more botanical and musical than pastoral. (He was indeed censured for neglect of humble parish matters, rushing services and omitting prayers in 1755-1757.) His efforts in other fields were not always appreciated by his parishioners!

By the time he became rector, at the age of 28, he had already established gardens and plantations at Gumley and Tur Langton. These had become local sightseeing attractions by 1754. He had collected seeds from all over world

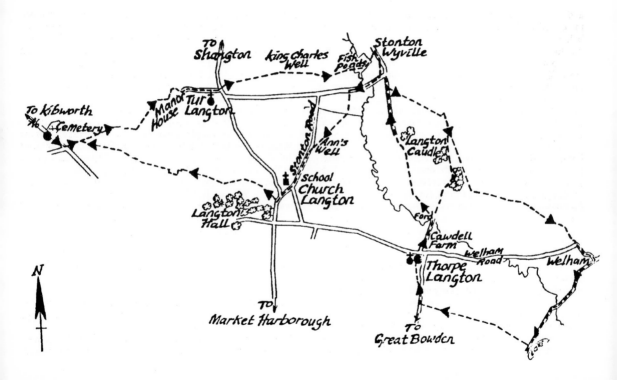

and set up a sort of Kew Gardens of his own. He planned to advertise his trees and plants to be sold annually. He believed large profits would accrue from scientific tree planting and he intended to put these profits 'to the Glory of God and the Advantage of Society'.

He published his Essay on Planting, in 1759: his History of the Rise and Progress of the Charitable Foundations at Church Langton in 1767: and his Encyclopaedia of Planting and Gardening in 1770. Concerned by loss of timber for naval ship building, he advocated one tree to be planted for each one cut down. (Compare this with our reponse to Dutch elm disease in the 1970s).

His musical activities were perhaps even more impressive: he organised the most spectacular musical festivals in 1759-1763. Hanbury himself gives us a very vivid picture of the grand occasion of the performance of Handel's Messiah in Church Langton on Sept 26th and 27th 1759: 2000 people were expected at 5/- a head. 200 coaches arrived in the village. Accommodation was so tight that stable rooms in Harborough were pressed into service and prices for fowl and butter tripled.

At 11.30 there was a solemn procession, followed by the performance: "and as few there had ever heard anything of that kind by such a band, most of them were struck into seemingly statues. Some of the common people were frighted and hurried out of the church for hearing of the kettle drums, which they took to be thunder and the trumpets sounding in the midst of such an heavenly noise of instruments, they thought of what had been reported,

that the Day of Judgment was really come indeed. The more judicious, however, were heightened into a true sense of devotion and declared they had never heard the service begin with such emotion and warmth of heart, or were so affected with it as they were at this time after being awakened into a sense of duty by so affectingly grand music".

(Handel himself attended the festival, staying with his librettist at Gopsall Hall.)

The interest on the profit from all these activities was to be applied to decoration of the church of Langton and to support an organist and schoolmaster. He also had grandiose plans for a rural university to be established at Church Langton, but died aged 52 before they could be achieved. (History of the Parish of Langton by John Harwood Hill 1867).

The beautiful Rectory which stands facing the green was built by his son William 1758-1817.

The alabaster monument medallion in his memory was erected in 1896 by his great grandson Rev Thomas Hanbury.

The Hanbury school was established for children of the parish in 1820-1884. The fine Victorian patterned red brick school was built in 1874 by Henry Goddard of Leicester. 70 boys and 50 girls were in attendance in 1875. It is now used as a school field centre.

Stonton Wyville. In 1628 Thomas Brudenall was created Baron Brudenell of Stonton and for many years the village was called Stonton Brudenell.

The former Fox and Hounds inn is now a private house near the church. Water Mill house still remains but the windmill which once stood on top of the Caudle is no more.

The little church of St Denys was restored in 1863 by Goddard of Leicester. Various monuments to the Brudenall family remain, including a stone tablet set in the external south wall of the nave dedicated to William Brudenell, gent., who died in 1636, aged 88.

Welham situated beside the river Welland, the border of Leicestershire at this point. In the early 18th century Francis Edwards, who owned land here, planned a new turnpike road from Leicester to London to pass through Welham. He built a large inn for expected travellers but the scheme fell through and the place was converted to a mansion and gardens. The walls of the ruins still stand, near the church. (Collinson)

Walk 12 – The Langtons

KIBWORTH · TUR LANGTON · STONTON WYVILLE · CHURCH LANGTON · KIBWORTH

7 miles gentle hill walking. A pleasant 4 hour stroll over mainly sheep pasture with fine views of all the Langton churches and the Caudle hills.

The walk could be extended from Stonton Wyville to Thorpe Langton and Langton Caudle, (3 miles), by adding on the next walk. You could also add on the 7 mile walk to Welham, from Stonton Wyville, to make a 14 mile figure of eight. Alternatively, you could shorten the walk by beginning at Tur Langton. (Instructions are given for returning to your starting point.)

Kibworth is situated about 8 miles south east of Leicester on the A6 to Market Harborough. There is a good lay bye south east of the village on the A6 opposite a little cemetery ground between the two roads leading to Kibworth Harcourt.

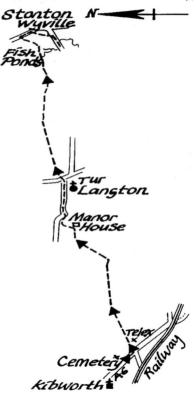

From Kibworth (to Tur Langton)
Walk along the A6 towards Market Harborough for 300 yards, passing the little cemetery on your left. A footpath sign on your left, opposite New Road, leads you into a field with a fenced off telephone exchange building in the right hand corner. Walk straight across this field, equi-distant between the two hedges on either side. Continue in the same direction in the next little field and in the following large field. Walk uphill to the brow of the hill, parallel with the hedge on your left.
A bridle gate near the left hand corner of the field gives you a good view of Tur Langton church spire, your next goal, straight ahead.
The path now takes you on a grassy unhedged track between crops. When it meets a hedge continue in the same direction, but move so that the hedge is on your left. Continue downhill in the direction of the church and cross the concrete farm bridge over the stream.

*Here you join the bridleway to Tur Langton which swings slightly left and goes uphill. Keep close to the hedge on your left until you reach the farm drive.

At this point you will see that the original line of the footpath was straight through the gate opposite between the Manor House and old church. It has now been diverted to take a big semi circular sweep to the left of the farm buildings and then right again to regain the line of the path at the corner of the drive to the old manor house.

Turn sharp left along the farm track for about 20 yards and cross the stile on your right into the field with old church remains. Keep close to the hedge on your left and cross the next stile which leads you back onto the farm track.

Pass the farm buildings on your right. Ignore the track to the road on your left and keep moving past the buildings on your right. Continue your semi circle round the farm until you are facing the tree lined avenue to the manor and then make for the left hand corner of the field where a

stile takes you onto the drive. Turn left along the drive to meet the village street. Turn right and walk through the village, passing the village hall and the Crown Inn on your left and the church on your right.

The Bulls Head stands at the T junction ahead and your path goes to the left of the pub, along a grassy lane. At the end of the lane you need to go through the gate and then turn right to cross the hedge. Turn left and walk with this hedge on your left through a very interestingly bumpy field with water-filled hollows of old sand and gravel workings. Keep close to the hedge on your left for two fields.

Near the bottom of the second field where the hedge juts out, cross the waymarked stile to the right of some ricketty sheep pens and walk with the hedge on your right. You are now walking due east, parallel with the road to Stonton Wyville but on high ground. The next crossing is about 30 yards to the left of the right hand corner. Walk along the crest of the hill for

two fields and cross the hedge about 100 yards left of the spinney. You should be close to the hedge on your right. Follow it downhill for two fields until you are about 100 yards from the stream in the valley. Cross through the hedge near the big ash tree.

Turn left and continue walking downhill towards the stream, with the hedge on your left. The footbridge is hidden within the stream bed about 30 yards from the left hand corner of the field.

On the far side of the stream lie the old fishponds of Stonton Wyville. Move slightly right and cross through the hawthorn hedge and walk along the fishpond banks close to the willow lined stream on your right. Move slightly left to pass the big house and meet the road beside the church in the left hand corner of the field. Turn right and walk along the road.

From the cross roads ahead you could add on a round trip of three miles to Thorpe Langton and the Caudle as described in the next walk before returning to Kibworth.)

To return to Kibworth (and Tur Langton) from Stonton Wyville (via Church Langton)

Turn right at the footpath sign opposite West View farm (between the church and the cross roads). Cross the field diagonally and cut off a corner of the road, which you meet again just to the left of Mill farm. Turn right and walk along the road for a quarter of a mile to pass two fields on your left.

Turn left at the footpath sign and walk with the hedge on your left to meet the stream.

Cross the bridge and make your way directly towards Church Langton church tower, crossing one wire fence and moving uphill to meet the road at a gate in the far right corner of the field. Walk up the road until you reach the church on your right and the school on your left. (Church Langton is full of interesting and beautiful buildings.)

Continue along this road, passing the village green and war memorial, until you come to the main B6047. Turn left along this road. There is a footpath sign directly opposite the Langton Arms pub.

Turn right and go through the kissing gate close to the farmhouse on your right. Walk with the farmhouse wall on your right, skirting the cattle pens. Cross the farm drive and the stile in the right hand corner of the field.

Continue to follow the farmhouse hedge on your right. When it ends, turn right and go to the corner of the field. Cross the waymarked stile, near a telegraph pole.

Turn left and follow the power lines. There is a stile crossing 30 yards to the right of the next telegraph pole.

Continue with the power lines to your left. Cross under them to meet a hedge corner. Walk with the hedge on your left and go through a series of stiles in a little fenced off area beside a spinney.

In the large field pass the isolated telegraph pole and walk in a straight line parallel with the hedge of West Langton Hall over to your left. The hedge on the right of this field swings away to the right, towards a copse of trees.

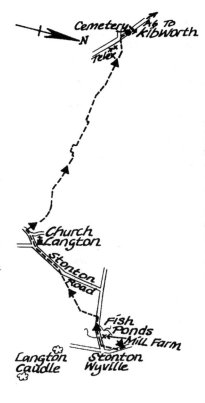

You should meet the hedge in front of you just to the left of a corner where the next field juts into this large one, about 200 yards south of the copse of trees on your right. Cross into the corner of the next very big field and go diagonally right, crossing a stream bed which lies in the dip, and go uphill towards a clump of trees on the skyline.

Continue in the same direction across the next field and go to the right of the clump of trees. Keep close to the hedge on your left. Your route actually goes to the isolated tree directly ahead, but the map indicates you should follow the hedge on the left, where it makes various right angled bends to reach this point.

Pass your marker tree in the hedge on your left and walk downhill to reach the stream and footplank ahead of you.

Here the bridleway crosses your path and goes right to join the path to Tur Langton which we took at the beginning of the walk.

(If you wish to return to Tur Langton without taking the last mile into Kibworth you can turn right here and swing right at the footbridge to bring you back on the route described earlier, on page 75 from Kibworth to Tur Langton.)

To continue to Kibworth, keep on in the same direction, but move to your left to walk uphill close to the hedge on your left. This field may seem a little tedious as it is sometimes ploughed right to the edge, and you begin to have sight and sound of the traffic of road and railway.

The gate at the end of the field is a little to your right. In the next field move slightly right to reach the hedge in the corner of the field ahead of you.

Turn right immediately and cut across the corner of the field. Cross through the hedge on your right and continue in the same direction, walking slightly away from the hedge on your left.

You are now crossing the same field that you crossed at the beginning of the walk. Kibworth church tower is ahead of you, in dark trees. The sails of Kibworth Post mill can be seen to the right of the church.

Cross through the hedge ahead of you (using the waymarked gap) and walk towards the telephone exchange enclosure. The footpath sign is just to the right of the buildings. Turn right along the A6. Kibworth cemetery ground laybye is 300 yards along the road.

**STONTON WYVILLE ·
THORPE LANGTON ·
LANGTON CAUDLE ·
STONTON WYVILLE**

A short stroll of $3\frac{1}{2}$ miles, which could be started from either Stonton Wyville or Thorpe Langton. In one direction you travel along a flat field road and in the other you climb up over the Caudle hill, which gives marvellous views over the surrounding countryside. If you start from Stonton Wyville you could add this short walk onto either of the other walks in this section.

Stonton Wyville is a tiny hamlet on the road between Kibworth and Hallaton, near Tur Langton. Thorpe Langton lies on the road between Kibworth and Welham, near Church Langton.

From Stonton Wyville crossroads, walk away from Stonton Wyville village and take the field road to Thorpe Langton.
This starts as a metalled track between hedges then becomes a well marked farm track until you reach the last field before the ford. This is waymarked as part of the Leicestershire Round.
In the last field, which descends to a stream, you need to leave the hedge on your right and move diagonally downhill to reach the ford. When this field is ploughed the farmer usually leaves a good headland and expects you to move round two sides of the field, turning left to follow the hedge on your left and then right to follow the hedge down to the ford.
There is a concrete bridge over the stream. If the water is high you might need to cross the hedge on your left to reach it.
Cross the bridge and walk up the lane to Thorpe Langton.
The Bakers Arms pub is to your left. The church is to your right.

From Thorpe Langton to Stonton Wyville via The Caudle
Go down the lane 'unsuitable for motors' at the left of the Bakers Arms. When you reach the ford, cross the concrete footbridge.

(Note the footpath sign to your left. This leads to the field road to Stonton Wyville. It is the 'low road' and we are about to take the 'high road'.)
Walk uphill with a hedge on your left. The field is a long 'corridor' which leads you up to the Caudle. Go through the gate in the narrow neck end of the field.
Here you need to leave the hedge on your left and go diagonally uphill. Follow the track through the woodland, keeping the main body of the wood to your right and go through a small stretch of thinner woodland to the open field ahead.
Keep in the same direction, moving slightly uphill, through another long narrow field, passing Langton Caudle spinney on your left. Cross the stile in the far left corner, close to the spinney. Walk uphill with the hedge on your left until you reach the trig point on your left at the top of the hill.
It is worth stopping to admire the views here. The churches of Church Langton, Thorpe Langton, Cranoe and Glooston can all be seen and you can pick out the Roman Road to

Slawston Hill, with Medbourne beyond. We now descend to Stonton Wyville by the same route that we used at the beginning of the first walk in this section.

Pass the trig point on your left and go to the corner of the field, keeping the hedge on your left. Turn left through the handgate and walk with the hedge on your right.

Cross through a gap on your right and continue to walk with this tall hawthorn hedge now on your left. At the end of the field

go through the handgate in the hedge opposite and continue in the same direction.

The path now leaves the hedge on your left and goes downhill to the far corner of the field where you meet the field road. Turn right and cross the main road to reach Stonton Wyville.

St Leonard's Church, Thorpe Langton

STONTON WYVILLE • LANGTON CAUDLE • WELHAM • THORPE LANGTON • STONTON WYVILLE

7 miles, over the Caudle Ridge, mainly pasture with some gentle lane and track walking.
Stonton Wyville is a small hamlet on the road between Tur Langton and Hallaton. It has no public facilities, but it is usually possible to park on the wide verge in the field road near the cross roads.

From the crossroads at the Stonton Wyville road junction. Walk away from Stonton Wyville village, along the field road which leads to Thorpe Langton.
Walk along the field road for 200 yards and turn left at the footpath sign. Go diagonally uphill across this big field to reach the top of the Caudle.
In the top left corner of the field there is a bridle gate. Keep in the same direction and walk with the hedge (of tall hawthorns) on your

right. At the end of the field you need to cross onto the right side of this hedge and walk with it on your left until you reach the corner of the field.
The trig. point which is your next goal can be seen ahead of you. To reach it you should continue to the corner of the field to go through the handgate and then turn right. Pass the trig. point on your right, pausing to admire the view.
Thorpe Langton is in the valley ahead of you, in line with the hedge on your right. We, however, are going to swing left and make our way along the top of the ridge, before descending to Welham.
Move away from the hedge on your right, and descend a little bank of rough ground. The right hand corner of the field dips down away from you (to Thorpe Langton) and you need to keep to the highest ground to reach the opposite hedge just to the left of a big tree, where a handgate brings you out into the corner of a long narrow field with a hedge on your right.

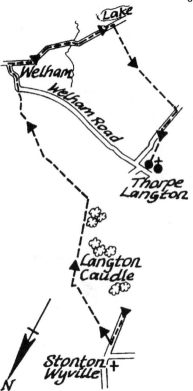

F

Walk 14 – The Langtons

Make your way across this long narrow field, keeping to the crest of the hill. (This can be quite hard going as the land is usually ploughed, but it is worth it for the views!) You should eventually reach the far left corner with a hedge on your left and a gate ahead of you.

From here you can see that if you continue in the same direction to reach the next gate you will then be swinging left to follow the high ridge.

Cross the little corner of the field. Go through this gate into the corner of the field. Turn left to walk with the hedge on your left. Keep the hedge on your left as you walk along the next two very long fields. (The second field has old water-filled gravel pits on your right.) As you descend to the third field you see a giant pylon ahead of you. Pass to the right of this pylon and cross the field diagonally, to the corner where you meet the road and go left to Welham.

(It is possible to cut the walk short here and return to Thorpe Langton by turning right along the road, but it is much prettier and not much further to go left and continue the walk via Welham.)

FROM WELHAM, with its squat towered church and its pub, turn right before you reach the church itself and walk along the road 'unsuitable for traffic', passing the walls of the Manor farm to your left.

Walk for 1 mile until you reach a lake on your left, just before a bend in the road. There is a stile for fishermen to the private lake on your left and a bridleway signpost on your right.

Turn right and walk along the lovely wide green lane which leads straight to Thorpe Langton. It is easy to follow, even though the hedge on your right has been removed in places. When you reach the road, turn right.

The road leads into Thorpe Langton but the prettier route is to leave the road after 200 yards and walk into the village by crossing a lovely pasture with interesting humps and hollows, aiming straight for the church spire. Keep to the right of the pond and follow the hedge on your left to reach a little handgate and stone steps which bring you out on a lane at the right of the church.

Pass the church on your left and join the main road of Thorpe Langton near the Bakers Arms on your right.

Glooston

Goadby (Gouti's by) Goadby village is on the western spur of the Keythorpe Wood hill where the ground rises to nearly 600 ft along the parish boundary. In the narrow valley immediately west of the village the boundary with Nosely parish follows a small stream which flows southward and eventually joins the Welland.
The village is small and compact. It consists of five farms, a few cottages and two larger houses grouped round a small triangular open space. Some new building is taking place near the church.   The small church stands in a little churchyard up a little lane, to the north of the street, immediately behind the Home Farm. It was probably founded as a manorial chapel in the late 12th or early 13th century. A tiny church door is inscribed "gift of William Collinson 1618".
Near the corner of the lane is the former National School built in 1857, closed in 1933 and now converted into a house. The front is faced with stone and has elaborate 'Tudor' features, including leaded windows with stone tracery and hood moulds. The Hazelrigg crest is above the doorway. Several of the houses also have connections with the Hazelrigg family.

Glooston (Glorstone in Domesday Book, Glor's Tun)
The church is Victorian, by Joseph Goddard, 1866, but the settlement is ancient. The village lies close to the Gartree Roman road, between Leicester and Medbourne, where Roman remains have been found. A Roman villa was discovered here.

There is a moat beside the lane which connects the village with the Gartree road.
The row of stone terraced cottages opposite the pub has recently been renovated most attractively.

Nosely 7 miles north of Market Harborough, the home of the Hazelriggs. At the time of the Conquest it was owned by the Martinall family, whose daughter Joyce married Sir Robert de Saddington. Their daughter Isabel married Ralph Hastings of Kirby and their daughter Margaret, who died in 1406, had a daughter who married Heselrige, a direct ancestor of the Hazelrigg of Civil War fame. Thus it has been in the same family since the Conquest and has never been sold. The private chapel has effigies of the Hesilriges 1220 -1305.

Tugby (Tochebi in Domesday Book, Tokebi 1190. Toki's by.)
12 miles from Leicester on the road to Uppingham. Hoskins describes the church as a most interesting example of early Norman building and includes it in his list of Excellent churches worth a visit. Pevsner says the church has a late Anglo-saxon base and a late Norman south doorway and a large and beautiful monument to Richard Neeld 1574. Arthur Mee mentions its rare Saxon window.

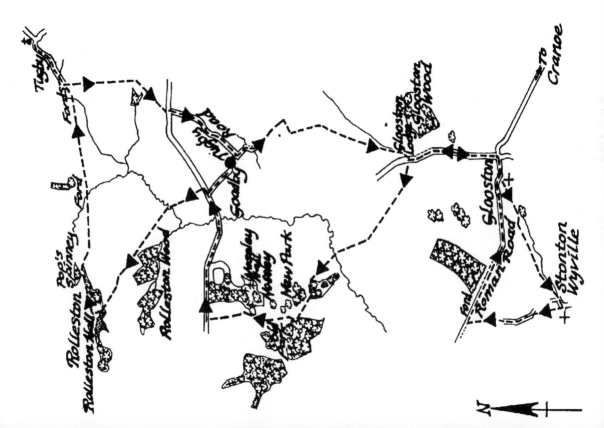

STONTON WYVILLE • GLOOSTON • STONTON WYVILLE • 3 miles.

A round trip which can be added on to any other of the walks in this section, beginning from Stonton Wyville.

From Stonton Wyville pass the church on your left and walk along the road. It is possible to walk to the end of this road to reach the gate into the field you want and then continue moving slightly right to reach the farm track, but the footpath route marked on maps takes you round the back of the houses on the right hand side of the road.

To follow the footpath, turn right up the drive of the first house. (This house is the old Fox and Hounds inn.) The path goes left, after you have passed the stable building, and passes the bottoms of the gardens. It goes across the level grass field, recently made into a tennis court. *The fencing around the tennis court obstructs the path and it would be advisable for the owners to way-*

mark the route they wish you to take to reach the gate ahead of you, slightly to your right.
Go through the gate (or cross the fence if you cannot reach the gate) and emerge close to a little pond in the field. Pass this on your left and walk straight up the very interesting humpy field to emerge at a bend in the farm track on your right. Cross the fence and continue in the same general direction along the track, walking northwards for three quarters of a mile until you meet the Roman Road (merely a grass track here) close to some barns at the top of the incline. There is a three way signpost, ($11\frac{3}{4}$ miles from Leicester, 1 from Glooston and 2 from Cranoe and 1 from Stonton Wyville.)
Turn right and walk along the Gartree road. This Roman Road leads you back to Glooston. Walk with the hedge on your left in the first field and continue in the same direction. The path becomes a hedged lane and swings slightly left, away from the line of the Roman road, just before Glooston.

You arrive in Glooston at the end of the village, with Glooston church on your right and the Old Barn restaurant just to the left of it. Here you take a U-turn to the right to return to Stonton Wyville.
The footpath goes between the church and the Roman road.

Glooston to Stonton Wyville
Pass the church on your left. Go through the gate beside the church and enter the field. Move slightly left towards a pylon. Pass just to the right of a small tree enclosure sewage works in the corner of the field. The path now goes in a straight line keeping the willow lined stream to your left. It begins by passing to the right of a pylon but it is waymarked in a way which directs you along the headland of the fields, close to the stream. When the land is ploughed you may find this easier. The crossing points are some fifty yards to the right of the stream.
After three fields emerge on the farm track. Turn left to reach Stonton Wyville church.

Walk 16 – Goadby

**GOADBY · GLOOSTON
LODGE · NOSELY · GOADBY ·
GOADBY · ROLLESTON ·
TUGBY · GOADBY**

A 9 mile figure of eight walk which can be taken in 2 walks of either 4 or 5 miles.
Goadby is a tiny village. The small church is tucked away at the end of a lane beside the old school. There are few other facilities apart from a phone and letter box, but it makes a pleasant starting point...

From Goadby village green pass the lane which leads to the church on your left and a telephone box on your right. Walk down to the T-junction and turn right (along the road signposted to Glooston 2 miles). Walk along this gated road, which immediately takes a sharp left turn. Go downhill, crossing the cattle grid, and then follow the road uphill (noting Nosely Hall over to your right). When the road bends right you need to go straight on. Cross the fence and walk steeply uphill. Pass a line of hawthorns on

your left and walk past an isolated ash tree on your right. Go over the fence in the gap in the hedge facing you.
In the next field there are farm barns and stable sheds. Pass to the right of these and emerge at a stile in the far left corner of the field, just past the new bungalow (Pine Tree Stud).
Turn right to meet the gated road again. Turn left and walk along the road (passing the field road to Hallaton on your left). Our next goal is Glooston Lodge.
The footpath leaves the road at the first cattle grid. (But if the field is obstructed by crops you could continue along the road. It is not much further. Glooston Lodge is the first house on your left.)
Where the road bends slightly right, near the cattle grid, the footpath continues straight ahead, moving across the field. Aim for the roof of Glooston Lodge, the red brick farmhouse which you can see through a gap in the hedge ahead of you. Cross through the gap in the hedge and go down to the

Walk 16 – Goadby

bottom corner of the field. Cross the poplar lined stream and turn right. Walk with the stream on your right. Pass the house and turn right to cross the cart bridge and walk up to rejoin the road, passing close to Glooston Lodge on your right.

From Glooston Lodge.
On the opposite side of the road to Glooston Lodge there is a big barn. To the right of this is a hedge and a gate. Go through the gate and walk with the hedge on your left.

At the end of the first field go through the gate and continue slightly right, walking up the shallow valley which leads to a tree-lined pond and aiming for the pylon which is on the skyline.

At the top of the field there are very fine views. You can see Nosely Hall beyond the valley ahead of you.

Go through the gate in the left side of the field corner. This takes you into a corner of the next field. Walk with the fence on your right and when it ends continue in the same direction to cut across a little corner to a hand gate.

Nosely Hall is slightly to your right ahead of you. Note an isolated tree in line with the hall and a little round spinney to the right. To the left of the tree note a spinney with a distinctive 'nose' sticking out. Our path goes from the isolated tree to the tip of this 'nose', but as the route is usually obstructed by crops you might need to make your way to the marker tree and thence to the 'nose' of the spinney by walking along the 'tram tracks' made by farm vehicles.

Go downhill to reach the stream and move slightly right to find a good brick bridge across it. This brings you out near the marker oak tree. Continue uphill passing close to the tree.

Pass the 'nose' of the spinney on your left and then swing left. Make for a gap between the spinneys on your left. (The gates have recently been waymarked by the Country Land-owners Association.)

Pass between the spinneys and turn right, making for the right hand corner of the wood ahead of you. Go through the gate and walk

Walk 16 – Goadby

across the parkland of Nosely Hall. Walk with the wood on your left for a short distance. When the wood bends left, continue straight ahead to a waymarked gate. (Nosely Hall is diagonally right of you.)

Follow the track until it swings right to enter the farm buildings in the wood, then continue straight ahead on the grassy track. In the next field the track becomes more faintly marked and it swings slightly left. Go through the gate to the left of a red brick wall and continue with a hedge on your right until you meet the road. Turn right and walk along The Avenue (a lovely tree lined road) passing the impressive stone eagle-topped gate posts guarding the gates to Nosely Hall.

If you are weary or wish to return directly to Goadby, you can turn right at the footpath sign under the power lines and walk uphill to meet the road half way up the hedge on your left, at the footpath sign. Turn right and walk along the road for a third of a mile. This makes a four and a half mile circuit.

To continue from Goadby to Rolleston and Tugby (the 9 mile circuit)
(Walkers from Goadby start here. Park in the village, walk a third of a mile to the Nosely-Tugby road junction and turn right to pass this farm on your left.)

From the Goadby turn on the Nosely-Tugby road walk towards Tugby for a short distance, passing a farm on your left. Turn left at the next hedge on your left and walk up the grass track between hedges. This is the bridleway to Rolleston. At the top of the lane you emerge in the corner of a field, where you make your way downhill diagonally right to a footbridge in a meander of the stream near the right hand corner of the field. This brings you out with a fence on your right. Head for Rolleston wood. Walk under the power lines. Continue in the same direction, crossing the next field diagonally, passing the corner of Rolleston Wood on your left. The gate in the corner of the field brings you out onto a well made track which takes you over

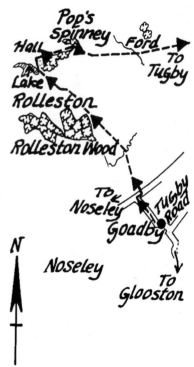

Walk 16 – Goadby

the hill, past farm buildings on your left and down towards Rolleston Lake, which you pass on your left.

Rolleston lake is a lovely spot, usually frequented by fishermen. If you wish to see Rolleston with its hall and private church, continue on this road and then return to the lake.

From Rolleston Lake to Tugby turn right at the first gate between the lake and Rolleston village. Walk with Pop's Spinney on your right. The track is well marked and goes in a due easterly direction all the way to Tugby.

At the end of Pop's Spinney cross the stream and follow the track as it swings slightly right uphill. Continue to the wide gateway ahead.

There are good views to your left over Skeffington Vale Farm and straight ahead of you in a big wooded hill you can see Keythorpe Hall.

Continue in the same direction, making your way downhill to the bottom right corner of the field, aiming for the right of a pylon. Go through the bridle gate in the bottom corner of the field and ford the stream, turn right and walk slightly away from the stream. Go

through a gap in the hedge ahead of you and walk with a hedge on your left for two long fields. Cross a dip where there is a stream to be forded in wet weather and continue with a hedge on your right. As you go uphill into Tugby you will see a gate on your right, by a stone cattle trough, which leads into a well marked track to Goadby.

If you wish to explore the delights of Tugby (which has a fine partly Norman church and two pubs which provide good food) you need to return to this point to continue the walk back to Goadby.

Walk along the track to Goadby with the hedge on your left through three more fields. Pass on your right a new made lake and at the next hedge turn right, leaving the solid track (which goes through a gap on your left). Walk with the hedge on your left.

When the hedge ends continue in the same direction along a grassy track, to emerge at the road junction by the signpost. Cross the road and walk half a mile into Goadby.

Pass Manor Farm and turn right to where you started the walk.

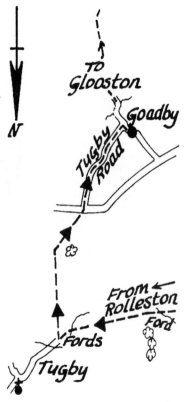

Hallaton

Hallaton lies 17 miles east of Leicester, 3 miles due south of East Norton and the A47 Leicester-Uppingham road, on the edge of the stone belt. The village contains an interesting mixture of stone and brick buildings. The oldest brick house is dated 1691 and brick was in general use from the 18th century onward.

It is the old stone thatched roof cottages, beautifully maintained, which give the village its picture book quality. It has three pubs where meals can be obtained, a duck pond, various shops and a small lock up (no longer in use!)

The church (of St Michael) is one of the most imposing of Leicestershire village churches.

Our walk crosses the stream, just to the south of the village, where the famous bottle-kicking contest takes place between the villages of Hallaton and Medbourne each Easter Monday, after the formal cutting and distribution of a hare pie at Hallaton Rectory. Each village attempts to gain possession of one or both of the two wooden 'bottles' or casks, which are hooped with iron and filled with ale. The origin of this custom, established in the 18th century at the latest, is unknown but presumably ancient. (J.B.Firth describes it in most unflattering terms: "Hallaton is best known throughout the shire for certain preposterous Easter Monday festivities which attract the vulgar from near and far.....Hare Pie scrambling is a silly and disgusting custom.... The Bottle kicking has at least some semblance of sport about it....There is no pretence at skill. It is just a mad rush over a quarter of a mile. Once over the brook the bottles are carried to the village cross; the corks are drawn, and the churned up ale is drunk".

Highways and Byways of Leicestershire, 1926 p.229)

Hallaton Hall stands on the east side of the village, its grounds surrounded by a high wall, occupying an island site between three roads. From 1713 until the middle of the 19th century it was the home of the Bewicke family. In 1958 it was occupied by nuns of the order of Our Lady of Good Counsel as a training school for novices and it was later a Toc H centre.

The green, which forms the centre of the village and is one of its most attractive features, is surrounded by old stone buildings. On it stands the Butter Cross, a conical stone structure with a circular base and a ball finial ('as ugly as useless', according to Firth!), probably dating from the late 17th century. Near it is the War memorial given by Mrs Bewicke in 1921 in memory of her son. The 'Bewicke Arms', a mid-17th century stone building with a steeply-pitched thatch roof, is at the south-east corner of the green. On the green's north side is a much-restored thatched cottage, formerly the smithy, and behind it stands the Conduit House. The Fox Inn at North End dates from the early 19th century. Dated tablets on buildings suggest that much modernisation was carried out by J.H. Dent in the mid-19th century. In Hog Lane, between High Street and Hunt's Lane, are six charity homes built in 1842 with an inscribed tablet in the centre gable. The village has a small local museum.

The motte and bailey Castle site is one of the finest in the county. The bailey was extensive and the ditch deep. Pevsner suggests that the purpose of the castle was to protect an iron-working site.

The dismantled railway line from Melton Mowbray to Harborough goes by the village. The station was closed in 1953.

Slawston The village lies over 300 ft and Slawston hill (also known as Mill, Barrow or Burrough Hill) exceeds 400 ft. Near the parish boundary with Medbourne is Port Hill. South of the parish the land is low and, being near the Welland, it is liable to flooding. The church of All Saints stands isolated at the east end of the village. It is made from ironstone and limestone and dates from the late 13th century, restored in 1864.
(Nicholls vol 2 part 2 p 795)

The parish was enclosed in 1793. In 1797 it is recorded there were in the village: 2 carpenters, 2 shoemakers, 2 millers, 2 shopkeepers, 1 blacksmith, 1 baker, 1 tailor, 1 barber, 1 victualler, 1 collarmaker, 7 woolcombers and 7 tammy weavers. (weavers of good quality worsted cloth with a glazed finish.) By the 1930s there was only 1 shop and an inn, the Black Horse. And now there are none....

There are no longer any facilities or shops in the village. The pretty little church lies to your left, at one end of the village, where there is, under a spreading chestnut tree, a seat donated by Mr Southgate, a grateful evacuee from Islington in appreciation of the kindness shown in 1940.

Cranoe Since the 16th century the greater part of Cranoe has belonged to the Brudenell family of Deene (Northants),subsequently Earls of Cardigan. Cranoe National School on the east corner of School Lane, was built of ironstone, and used to carry the date 1843 and the arms of Lord Cardigan on the central gable. The school was designed by the rector John Harwood Hill (1809-86) and erected by the 7th Earl of Cardigan (d.1868) for the use of children in four parishes where the Brudenell estates lay - Cranoe, Stonton Wyville, Glooston and Slawston. It is now a private house. There used to be one public house, the "Cardigan Arms" at the cross-roads on the east side of the Glooston road.

The church of St.Michael stands above and to the north of the village. It was severely damaged by a storm in 1846 and the rector took the opportunity of rebuilding the body of the church in 1846-9. The base of the tower is of the 13th-century with additions of the 15th or early 16th century. And there is a Norman font.

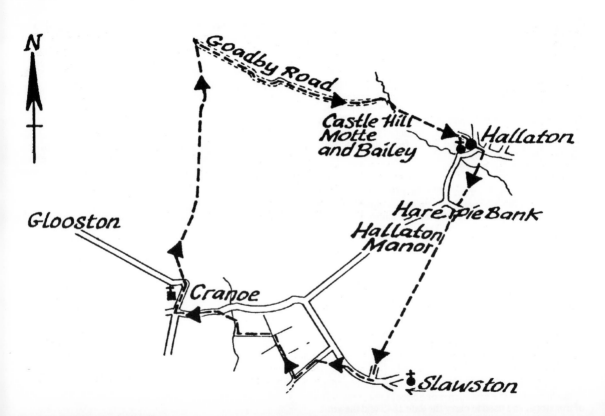

Walk 17 – Hallaton

**HALLATON · SLAWSTON ·
CRANOE · HALLATON ·
7 miles**

Beginning over pasture lowland
close to the Welland valley and
rising to high plateau farmland,
returning by track to the very pretty
village of Hallaton.
*Hallaton is a sizeable village about
17 miles from Leicester, 3 miles
south of East Norton on the
Leicester-Uppingham road.*

From Hallaton church walk along
towards the village green on which
stand the butter cross and the war
memorial. Just before you reach the
green, a footpath sign directs you to
an archway on your right between
two tall impressive houses, one of
which bears the date 1715.
Walk through the archway onto a
walled grassy track. This takes us
downhill to the concrete footbridge
over the stream.
Walk uphill with the wood on your
right and continue in the same
direction (parallel with a hedge over
to your left). At the top of the hill

pass a line of stumps of old large
tree trunks still visible on your left.
There is a gate in the top corner of
the field beyond the line of horse
chestnut trees on your left.
Cross the lane. The next field is
Hare Pie Bank field. Hallaton
Manor, an impressive stone house,
stands in front of you and you need
to go diagonally left, away from
the house.
Go downhill to the bottom right
corner of this lovely big meadow.
Cross the footbridge. You will be
making straight for Slawston
church spire, which stands to the
right of Slawston Hill.
Cross into the next field and
continue diagonally in the same
direction. You will now be moving
to the right of the church spire. The
crossing point should be just to the
right of a telegraph pole, but it is
probably easier to cross through
the farm gate a bit further along to
your right.
Continue in the same line, going
diagonally over the next field. In
the corner of the field are two gates
with footbridges over the stream.

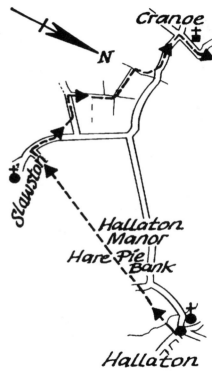

Select the one on the right and continue in the next field by walking close to the hedge on your left. At the end of this field move right and go through the kissing gate which is about 50 yards to the right of the field corner. Continue close to the hedge on your left until you come to a little handgate. This leads onto a green track between hedges, into Slawston village street.

From Slawston our path goes right, along the village street, to the end of the village. Pass Manor farm and find the footpath sign on your left, 50 yards further on.
Cross the stile and move diagonally right to where the hedge on the right ends. Pass a little pond on your left and continue across the corner of the field to a (waymarked) gate in the bottom corner. (Pass a little electricity sub station in the right hand corner of the field.) You now meet Occupation Lane.
The path used to go directly across the lane and continue in the same diagonal direction to the far corner of the next large field.

The route has recently been changed so that you need to walk left, along Occupation Lane and then right along the field edge to meet this point. There should be a good headland left to make for easy walking.
Turn left to reach the bottom of Occupation Lane. Turn right and walk close to the hedge on your left. Just before the corner of the field a double plank footbridge in the hedge on your left takes you into the corner of the field on your left and once again you need to walk two sides round the field to reach the crossing point. (At the end of the field turn right, keeping the hedge on your left.) Look for the footbridge in the hedge on your left, just past the first of a series of ash trees. Cut across the corner of the next field, moving to your right, making for the footpath sign. Go through the gate onto the road by the footpath sign. Turn left and walk along the road to Cranoe village. The church can be seen slightly uphill to your right.

At Cranoe crossroads, by the telephone box, turn right and walk up the quiet lane to the church. Pass between the church on your left and the (much extended) Old Rectory on your right. As the road bends left, behind the church, go through the gate ahead of you. Ignore the Leicestershire Round waymark sign pointing right and walk uphill close to the hedge on your left. At the end of the first field go through the gate beside the conker trees.
From the high ground here you have an impressive view of the Welland valley behind you and the Langtons to your left. Church Langton tower stands out clearly.
You now need to follow the hedge which goes in a straight line ahead of you but leading slightly to your right. (You should keep to the right of this hedge, but it is often easier to walk on the left side of it, where there is usually a good wide solid farm track. You can cross back when it is convenient and continue, with the hedge on your left.)
Continue in this line for a mile, across the top of the high plateau.
Here you have fine views over the

Walk 17 – Hallaton

wide countryside around. It has hills and little patches of woodland and, unlike the rest of the walk, there is not a village in sight. There are scarcely any farm buildings, either!
When a gate leads you into an open field keep in the same direction. (More or less parallel to the hedge over to your right.) Cross the wire fencing and continue in the same direction, until you find yourself eventually walking beside a hedge on your right.

At the end of this long field the hedge swings right slightly (where the remains of the red roof and walls of derelict Cranoe Lodge can be seen in the hollow on your left). Make for the gate ahead of you which brings you into the next field with the hedge on your left.

Continue with the hedge on your left until you reach the field road track on your right.

This is actually the County Road from Goadby to Hallaton. For a lovely view over to Nosely Hall and woods it is worth turning left along the track to look over the gate.

Turn right and walk along the track to Hallaton. This takes you back across the arable plateau and then winds down with a hedge at first on your left and then on your right. It becomes a beautiful lane with hedges on each side. A steep gulley on your right has been most attractively planted with trees and there are wild flowers in profusion. Cross the ford and footbridge. Continue along the lane, passing Castle Hill on your right. As you climb the hill you get good views of this impressive Norman motte and bailey.

At the top of the hill where the lane swings sharp left, go through the gate facing you and continue straight into Hallaton, making for the church spire, walking close to the hedge on your left.

Cross the stile in the corner of the field and continue uphill to reach the footpath sign and kissing gate in the corner of the field, just past a little graveyard on your right. Walk into the village, passing the lovely church of Hallaton on your right.

Belton in Rutland (not to be confused with Belton near Shepshed!) stands on the side of a steep hill about half a mile north of the main road from Leicester to Uppingham, which is about three miles away. The village was formerly within the bounds of Leighfield Forest and the name means the Tun in a glade in the forest.

On the green is a stone obelisk which forms the war memorial, the base of which, called the King's Stone, is said to have been a stone on which Charles 1 sat after the battle of Naseby.

The Old Hall, near the church, with remains of Tudor work, was probably the manor house and the site of the house where the Blounts lived in the 14th century. The present house was probably built by the Hazelwoods in the sixteenth century.

The village has had some narrow escapes. It was practically destroyed by fire in 1776 when 27 houses were completely burnt. In 1942 four large bombs were dropped from a Dormier 217 and The Black Horse and other houses in Chapel Lane were damaged: no people were injured but a pig was buried under the rubble.

Allexton A tiny village beside the Eye Brook, which is at this point the frontier with Rutland. The church of St Peter is basically late Norman (1160-80). The Hall was originally Elizabethan, later converted to a farmhouse and partly taken down in 1843, and then rebuilt in 1902. The grounds are famous for fine avenues of Balm of Gilead trees. (Hoskins, Shell Guide.)

East Norton has been promised a by-pass as the bends of the A47 through the village prove so dangerous at present. When it is built one might be able to walk along the village street once more to look at the 1643 house opposite the old Police Station.

The dismantled railway line crosses the A47 just east of the village, where it formerly went through a deep cutting and then through a tunnel on its way south to Medbourne and Market Harborough. The land has now been levelled but you can still pick out where it used to be.

Wardley (Old English weard, a watch place, and leah, a clearing in wooded country.)
There was a church here in Saxon times. Edward the Confessor granted the church of Wardley to Westminster Abbey. The south doorway dates from about 1175. The north door dates from about 1200. (Pevsner)

The small village served the Fludyer family of Ayston Hall. The well water supply at Wardley was so bad that when diphtheria developed in 1913 the Fludyer family installed a hydraulic ram to pump water from a spring in the valley. The supply continued in use for many years. (Rutland History Society pamphlet 1975.)

Wardley Hill has long been dreaded as a hazard by drivers along the Uppingham Road especially in winter when the snow piled up and vehicles of all sorts failed to negotiate the steep and icy bends. A new wide road has now been provided, avoiding the steepest part of the hill and protected from the worst of the icy blasts of winter.

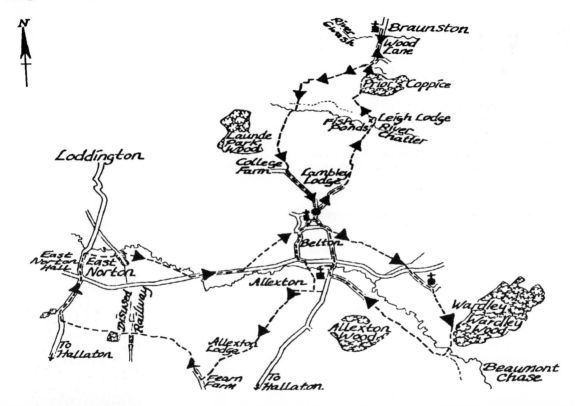

The tarmac surface of the old road which used to go from Wardley village to the former Uppingham road has been removed and it has reverted to a mere track. The old Uppingham Road, once such a busy death trap, is now a country lane.

Braunston (Brantestone in Domesday Book: Brand's village (probably some 9th century Danish overlord, according to Hoskins).
A lovely ironstone village snuggling in a valley about 3 miles south east of Oakham. The 15th century church has earlier Norman remains, including a massive Norman doorway and font. There are two pubs and a shop to provide refreshment and a spreading chestnut tree to shelter you on the village green.
The village was obviously once a centre for many pathways. It lies on the routes between important religious foundations. About a mile NW of the village on a hill rising from the river Gwash there are signs of earthworks extending towards Flitteris park. Hoskins suggests there might be a lost village here. One mile west of Braunston is the site of Brooke Priory and earthworks.

Walk 18 – Belton

BELTON • ALLEXTON • EAST NORTON • BELTON • 7 miles (to which you could add the 4 mile loop to WARDLEY if you wanted a slightly longer walk.)

Belton is situated beside the A47 Uppingham road 5 miles west of Uppingham and 18 miles from Leicester. The village makes a good start as it has 2 pubs, a tea place craft centre with miniature animals, lovely old stone houses and a church.

This is a walk to be undertaken when crops are low as the paths in this area are not well maintained, even where they are well way-marked! When once you reach the high ridge the walking is easy, over grass land with lovely views over the surrounding countryside.

From Belton church there are two roads leading down to the A47. Take the westerly one (New Road). Cross to the far side of the A47, and turn left, passing the lodge gates of Allexton Hall, on your right. Cross the stile which is just to the left of the lodge garden.

In the field, move slightly away from the lodge garden and cross the metal footbridge over the Eyebrook stream. Continue in this direction, moving towards Allexton church. To the right of the church there is a kissing gate beside a farm gate in the top left corner of the field. Emerge on the road near the post box in Allexton village.
Continue in the same direction, crossing the drive which goes between the church on your left and Allexton hall on your right. Go uphill past the village green with houses on each side of you.
The road becomes a little green lane (often overgrown and sometimes rather wet underfoot). At the top of the lane turn right and walk with the hedge on your right until you are level with Allexton Hall on your right. Here you turn left and follow the waymarked Leicestershire Round route to Fearn Farm.
Move uphill, away from Allexton Hall, with the hedge on your right, to a point where the hedge ends

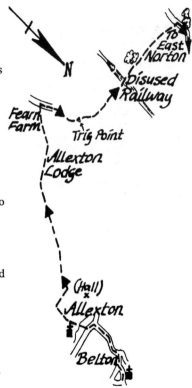

and a fence begins. There is a gate a little further up the hill, by a telegraph pole, which enables you to cross into the field on your right. Now make for Allexton Lodge farmhouse up on the hill in front of you. You need to go diagonally across the next fields.

Cut off the corner of the first field by walking down to the bottom hedge. The crossing point should be to the right of a pair of isolated trees, but as it is usually obstructed with barbed wire, it may be easier to go to the right and cross through the field gate.

Still making for the farmhouse, continue diagonally right up the next large field looking for a point about halfway up the hedge on your right, where there is a hedge junction. Cross at the waymarked stile just past this hedge junction and go diagonally uphill across the rough field, crossing a waymarked wire fence, to reach the gate at the left of Allexton lodge farm.

There are lovely views from this point and you deserve a little rest!

Pass the farm buildings and turn right to pass in front of the house, crossing the concrete drive, to reach two gates near some power lines. Go through the gate way and walk downhill with the hedge on your left, to the handgate at the end of the field.

Continue in the same direction uphill across the corner of a field to reach the waymarked gate.

Fearn Farm is on the hill ahead of you. To reach it, go over the hump of the field and then down through a gap near two trees and up the hill to a stile at the right of the farm.

At Fearn Farm turn right and walk uphill along the lane. Go through the left gate and continue with the hedge on your right up to the top of the field. Swing left, keeping the hedge on your right. (Ignore the gate). Pass a triangulation post.

You now have a beautiful high ridge walk with fine views all round you.

Keep walking with the hedge on your right and cross over the old railway line tunnel. (It is worth stopping to see the line of the old track and to note where it used to emerge at East Norton station on your right.)

Your path now becomes a well surfaced field road and emerges on Moor Hill, the road between Hallaton and East Norton. Turn right and walk over the hill and down into East Norton.

This short stretch of road walking gives you a lovely view over East Norton village. East Norton is unfortunately split in two by the A47 road, which spoils your chances of a pleasant bit of exploration of a pretty village.

You need to cross the Main A47 road and continue downhill.

Pass the beautiful wooded gardens of East Norton Hall on your left and continue downhill to the bend in the road. Turn right at the bridleway sign. This takes you across an interesting pasture field, full of humps and hollows. You are now walking due east with the Eyebrook river on your left, making for the impressive railway viaduct.

Keep on the high track (ignoring the well marked route closer to the stream below you. This is a route taken by

Walk 18 – Belton

horse riders, who go through the gap in the hedge ahead).

The high track leads you to a handgate just to the left of the power lines. This brings you out in the corner of the next field. You should then walk with the hedge on your left until you reach the handgate on your left at the end of the field.

Turn left and go through the hand gate and walk close to the railway cutting wood on your right.

A handgate ahead of you takes you into a little spinney path close to the railway bridge arch. (The well marked horse route goes below you on the flat land under the arch).

Follow the spinney path and emerge through the handgate at the far side. Continue following the hedge on your right. (The Eyebrook river is away to your left). Go through the farm gate and walk with the hedge on your left for three more big fields, passing farm buildings on your right and gradually meeting the Eyebrook on your left and the A47 on your right. As you approach the A47, leave the riverside and walk across the field to the signposted gate on the

Uppingham road. Turn left and walk along the A47. (Sorry about that, folks!)

There is a laybye on the right of the road where a caravan announces it is Maggies Sit-In Cafe, on the Rutland border. If it were open it would be worthy of custom. (It has always been closed whenever I have passed it!) From the laybye, just to the right of Maggies cafe, a farm gate leads to a very pleasant bridleway to Allexton. But the last time I walked it it was so obstructed by crops of rape and broad beans that I decided I couldn't possibly include it in this book! Hence the short stretch of road walking which follows:

You now need to close your ears to the sound of the A47 traffic and walk along the roadside verge. Pass the Rutland Inn on your left (it serves morning coffee and tea as well as alcohol). At the next field gateway turn left.

You should now aim directly towards Belton church tower, nestling in trees on the village hill. You have four lovely pasture fields

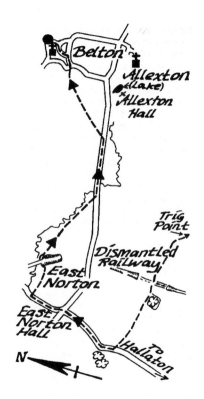

between you and Belton village but before you reach them you may have a small problem. You need to cut across the corner of a small arable field. You should reach the hedge ahead of you at a fence about 60 yards from the road. Continue in the same direction. The next crossing point is just to the left of a large ash tree. Now make your way up to the top left corner of the field. A ricketty fence brings you out by a small corner of the next field.

Walk downhill parallel with a hedge on your left. (There are good views of Allexton Hall over to your right.) The crossing over the stream is directly ahead of you and you are making for a point straight ahead in the next field. But there is no bridge over the stream at this point and you may find it easier to go through the handgate in the left hand corner of the field and then move uphill slightly right to reach the top corner of the next field. Walk close to the hedge on your right as it bends right to meet Main Street, Belton, by a footpath sign on New Road.

(The craft centre tea rooms are to your right. Here, when you have cleaned up a bit, you can purchase a very elegant cream tea.)

To return to Belton church and war memorial, where the walk started, walk along Main Street and turn left at Church Street, The Sun pub is on your right (It also serves meals) and the post office and general store up the road on your left.

Walk 19 – Belton

BELTON · WARDLEY · BELTON

A delightful short walk of 4 miles, mainly on tracks and well marked paths. The first section, from Belton to Wardley, is less easy and there is one rough, rather boggy field to negotiate but once you reach the old road to Wardley all is very plain sailing. This would make a delightful summer evening walk.

From Belton church and the war memorial, walk down Nether Street and follow Littleworth Lane for a short distance. Turn left at the footpath sign on your left, where the power lines cross the road.
A gate on your right takes you away from the small sewage works ahead of you. Cross the field diagonally to reach the bottom right corner. Ignore the cart bridge ahead of you and cross the fence and footbridge on your right. Walk with the stream on your left for 100 yards then turn left to cross the substantial wooden bridge. Walk parallel with the hedge on your right. At the end of

the field you need to cross a minor tributary stream. Cross the footbridge in the corner of the field. Walk with the hedge on your left in the next field and go uphill to a point where the hedge take a sharp right hand bend. Go through the gap and over the footbridge here. *Belton church tower is directly behind you at this point and Wardley church spire is straight ahead of you, at the end of a lime tree avenue of trees lining the edge of the old road leading into Wardley. This is your next goal.* The next field is almost invariably ploughed and obstructed and an alternative route has been proposed to replace the old straight line to Wardley church. The alternative route involves swinging right to follow the hedge on your right until you reach a corner where you are directly in line with the line of lime trees and Wardley church is just in front of you.
Now comes the rough field with a stream in the dip. It is a lovely

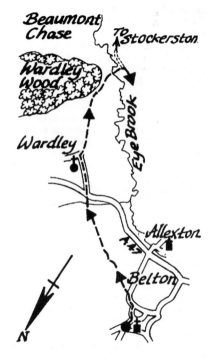

Walk 19 – Belton

neglected gulley with lots of wild flowers and butterflies, in summer, but it is also rather wet underfoot and it's a steep climb up to the old road. (The old footpath crossing is 200 yards to your left and may still be an easier place to cross the stream.) Cross the old Uppingham Road and walk with the lime trees on your left until you reach the new wide, fast and furious A47 by-pass to Wardley Hill. Cross this road as best you can and continue on the road into Wardley village.

The route is now delightfully easy. Pass the church on your left and swing right at the fork in the road. Go over the cattle grid and pass the big house on your left. Follow the track past the house and down to the right. Wardley Wood is in front of you and you are making for the right hand side of it. Go down to cross the stream and then turn right and left almost immediately, still following the track. This surfaced track takes you straight towards the wood and then turns right beside a hedge before turning left again to come close to the wood.

Walk close to the wood on your left

for a short distance. When you reach a gate on your left you will see a clear track which comes through Wardley wood. Here you need to turn right to go through a series of farm gates and across a cart bridge over the Eye Brook to reach the Allexton Field road. (If the field is obstructed by crops, continue to the next hedge and follow the headland round to the bridge and then continue to the road.)

The road goes left to Stockerston and Eyebrook reservoir (this adds 3 miles to the walk).

To return to Belton, turn right to walk along the quiet field road all the way into Allexton village. At the T-junction turn right, along the Hallaton road. At the next T-junction turn right again and swing left to cross the bridge. You now need to cross the A47 Uppingham Road (near the bus stop and phone box) to reach Belton. Walk up Littleworth Lane. Continue up Nether Street to the war memorial and church, where you started the walk.

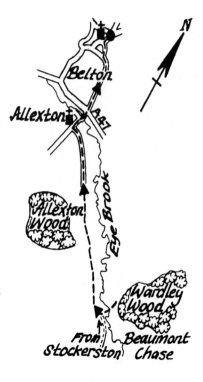

Walk 20 – Belton

BELTON · LEIGHFIELD · BRAUNSTON · BELTON ·
8 miles

This is a lovely walk crossing through the old Leighfield Royal Forest (now, alas, no more!) over long rolling waves of ridged hills which separate the river valleys of the Chater and the Gwash. These flow west-east and your path goes north-south to Braunston and back. The route is for the most part on farm tracks or surfaced lanes, but there are some forays into fields. The walk can easily be shortened if you wish.

From Belton church pass the war memorial and walk along Chapel Street. Take the right hand fork (to Lambley Lodge, No Through Road) along the metal surfaced road and continue in a generally northerly direction. After three quarters of a mile the road swings left, to Lambley Lodge but you need to go straight on with the hedge on your left.
At the T-junction at the top of the

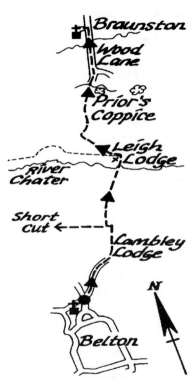

hill there is the most spectacular view down from the ridge over-looking the valley. In front of you lies the area which was the old Leighfield forest.
It is now arable farmland.
Turn left and walk to the farm buildings. (If you want to make a very short walk you can go straight ahead at this point along the Ridlington Ridge and return to Belton by omitting the following two pages.)
At the farm buildings turn right and walk with the hedge on your right. Walk along the farm track which descends very gently to Leigh Lodge, an impressive stone mansion on the site of the medieval hunting lodge with fish ponds on either side.
Near the bottom of the hill the track swings right and then left to cross the river Chater. Pass Leigh Lodge on your left. The track swings round behind the house. Here you meet a farm road which goes uphill to your right.
(If you wish you can take this hard surface route, which passes to

the east of Priors Coppice wood, all the way into Braunston, turning left at the first junction and right at the second to reach Braunston village. But this involves rather a lot of road walking. The footpath route is prettier. It crosses two big arable fields and then goes along the west side of Priors Coppice. The first two fields are rather hard going, I'm afraid, but the route beside the wood is delightful.)

To continue on the footpath route, cross the farm track and pass the back of Leighfield Lodge. In the corner of the next field, strike uphill diagonally crossing the highest part of the hill to the far left corner of the field. Then turn right and go through the gap in the hedge, to walk with the hedge on your left.

Cross the track at the top of the hill (an excellent viewing point) and walk downhill with the wood on your right.

At the bottom of the hill, where the wood swings right, a good track goes off to your left. (This is a useful escape route onto Wood Lane if the next part of our route is obstructed by crops or ploughed land.) To follow the correct route, ignore the track on your left and continue uphill to cross the field diagonally, making for the left of three trees ahead of you over the brow of the hill. Cross through the hedge at a fence crossing by the trees and continue in the same direction to the top left corner of the next field where you meet Wood Lane at the footpath sign. *At this point you can decide whether you wish to go into Braunston village, which lies to your right, half a mile along Wood Lane. If you wish to shorten the walk, you can omit the next two paragraphs describing the route into Braunston and back and continue from this point. The return route from Braunston to Belton lies left along the lane. We shall be returning to this point after our visit to the village.*

Turn right and walk down Wood Lane into the village of Braunston. There are two good pubs in the village and an ice cream shop and general store. The village makes a very picturesque spot for a picnic.

To return from Braunston to Belton
From Braunston pass the church on your right and walk with the stream on your left to go south along Wood Lane. After a quarter of a mile take the right fork and follow this lane for about 100 yards to the point where you emerged on it earlier (at the footpath sign).

Keep in the wide grass drift between hedges until you reach the end of the lane. Continue with the hedge on your left until you reach the end of the field. Turn right and go to the gate in the corner of the field. Turn left through the handgate. Meet the wide farm track and turn right to follow it as it moves west along the ridge. *At the end of the first field there is a concrete base of an old wind pump on your left. This is a good place to stop to admire the views. You can see on a fine day, Ridlington and Uppingham on the far ridges and a glimpse of Rutland Water to the east and Knossington mast to the north. And below, Leigh Lodge with its fish ponds.*

The OS Pathfinder line of the path goes from a gap in the hedge near the wind pump base and swings left to go diagonally left downhill to join a farm track but the land is almost always ploughed and it is much easier to continue along the wide track you have just walked along, keeping close to the hedge on your right, following the ridge until you see, in the field after the wind pump base, a clump of trees around a pond.

This is the point where you leave the ridge track. Turn left and walk along the farm track, passing the pond on your right.

You can now see the track winding its way up the hill ahead of you. As you descend the hill you can see Leigh Lodge in the river valley, to your left and Launde Park wood on the hill in front of you to your right.

Walk downhill until you reach the river Chater. Swing right to cross the bridge. Pass a spinney on your left and continue on the track as it swings left to go uphill.

At the top of the hill, where the land falls away from you, there is a cross ways of paths. (The Ridlington ridge track comes in from your left.) You need to continue downhill, close to the hedge on your right.

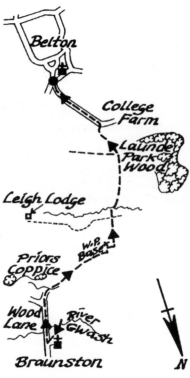

The Eyebrook reservoir can be seen ahead of you here, and you may get a glimpse of Rutland Water to your left. Go downhill with the hedge on your right for 60 yards and then swing leftish on a well marked track (parallel with a hedge on your right at the bottom of the hill).

Go through the gate ahead and walk with the hedge on your left in the next field. Follow this hedge as it swings right to meet the bridle gate on the lane. Turn left and walk along the lane (from College farm to Belton) for a mile. Emerge in Belton beside the Baptist chapel. Continue straight ahead along Chapel Street until you reach the church.

Burrough Hill

Burrough Hill commands a wide view of the Wreake valley. The trig point here is at 690 feet, and it seems quite a strenuous climb up from the base but in fact the hill is not quite as high as Robin a Tiptoe (726 feet) or Whatborough Hill (758 feet).

The Iron Age hill encampment was probably a settlement about four hundred years before the Romans came to Britain. The fortifications and the gateway entrance were probably added in about 300 B.C. When the Romans arrived the native British Coritani tribe were in possession. Romano-British pottery has been found on the site, showing that it was used in Roman times but it is likely that it was abandoned soon after the Roman invasion.

The walls are about 28 feet high in places and 44 feet thick at the base. Excavations at the south side of the entrance revealed a cobbled road surface and a guard house. (Shell/County Trust Nature trail leaflet).

Leland writing in the 16th century records that: 'to these Borow Hills every year on Monday after Whit Sunday come people of the country thereabout, and shoot, run, wrestle, dance, and use like other feats of exercise'. Ogilvy writing in 1675 reports the same activities. Burton writing in 1622 quotes Camden as describing the hill as: "a ploughed field remarkable for nothing so much as the sports practised here yearly by the neighbouring youth". (Nicholls II.ii 524). These sports apparently continued intermittently until the 18th century.

In the 19th century the Melton Hunt established a race meeting there on the Wednesday after the second Sunday in June. These races were held until about 1870.

The hill is now preserved and maintained as a public amenity by Leicestershire County Council.

Burrough on the Hill lies on the western edge of the uplands of east Leicestershire, about 12 miles north-east of Leicester. The oldest parts of the church probably date from the early 13th century. The church path is lined with old stone grave stones.

Ironstone is the predominant building material in the village and many of the houses date from the 18th and early 19th centuries. Earlier buildings include two small 17th century farmhouses (The Limes and Cheselden Farm) and some 17th century houses on south east of the main street. Opposite the church is a tall brick house known as the Manor, built in 1781 probably by Robert Peake. By the early 20th century there were 3 large houses in the parish used as hunting boxes or occupied by hunting families.

(1) Burrough Hill House, built in 1876 by C.W.Chaplin.

(2) Burrough House, a former farm house in the village street near the lane to Owston.

(3) Burrough Court which formerly stood half a mile from the village on the road to Twyford, built c.1905 by H.C. Allfrey, later used as a hunting box by Marmaduke, Viscount Furness (d.1940). Between the world wars it became a well-known meeting place for the hunting society of Melton; in the autumn of 1930 the first meeting between Edward, Prince of Wales, and Mrs Wallis Simpson (late

Duke and Duchess of Windsor) took place there. The house was burnt down during the Second World War when it was requisitioned for troops.

There is one inn, the 'Stag and Hounds', an early-19th century building at the south-west end of the village. The John O'Gaunt railway hotel was converted to a private house in 1958 and the railway station is now an industrial site.

The railway line from Bottesford to Market Harborough was opened in 1879 and the station of John O'Gaunt was built a mile away from the village on the Twyford road. The station was named after the nearby John O'Gaunt fox covert. The railway line was dismantled in 1953 although the great viaducts still stand as testimony to its former glory.

Burton Lazars *2 miles North west of Melton, 8 from Oakham, 14 from Leicester.*

The hospital was built (according to Nicholls) by subscription "a general collection throughout England" in 1135-1154 during the reign of King Stephen. (The Victoria County History thinks this unlikely and gives the credit to Roger de Mowbray, who fought in the second Crusade in 1147.) It was so rich a foundation that all the inferior Lazar houses in England were in some measure subject to its master, as he himself was to the Lazars at Jerusalem. It provided for a master and 8 sound and several poor leprous brethren of the order of St Augustine.

Gifts of land from local worthies included Sir John Digby of Tilton "for the health of his own and his ancestors soules."

William Burdett in 1184 gave them the hospital of Tilton (Query; could this have been at Halstead?) and land at Cold Newton and church dues at Lowesby and Gaulby. The hospital was exempted from tax. (Nicholls 1800 Framland volume.)

Somerby (*Sumerledebi   Summerdebie in Domesday Book, from the Old Norse Sumerlidi's bi, the summer warrior's by.*) *Somerby Hall*, now demolished, was once the home for dashing Fred Burnaby a 'thoroughly English type of man, robust, conservative, aristocratic soldier, opaque in intellect but indomitable in muscle'. (Firth, *Highways and Byways*). There is a memorial window to him in the church and to his father who was vicar. He was the author of a famous Victorian travel book, *The Ride to Khiva*, and died fighting Arabs in the Sudan.

Little Dalby The churchyard makes a lovely picnic peaceful picnic stop. If you walk quietly you might see a kestrel perched on the buttress. The hall is just beyond the church and has a gravelled path leading to it, through iron handgates.

Step 10 • Burrough Hill

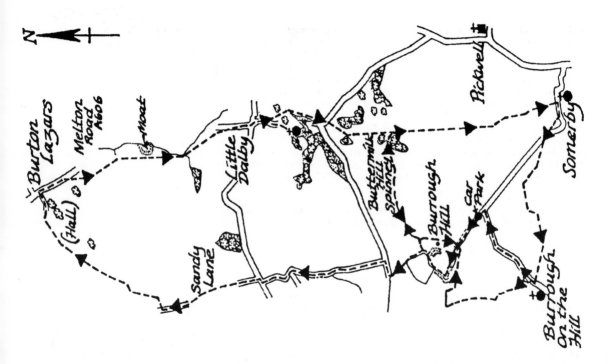

N

Burton Lazars
Melton Road A606
Moat
(Hall)
Little Dalby
Sandy Lane
Buttermilk Hill Spinney
Burrough Hill
Car Park
Pickwell
Somerby
Burrough on the Hill

BURROUGH HILL · BURTON LAZARS · BURROUGH HILL · 8½ miles.

You could start the complete walk either from Burrough Hill or from Burton Lazars, choosing to start with the section which suits you best. (It's satisfying to start in the flat plain of Burton Lazars and climb to the high point of Burrough Hill, but Burrough Hill has the better car parking facilities and may be nearer for you to get to.

From Burton Lazars the route goes through Little Dalby and thence gradually up along the Dalby Hills to the foot of Burrough Hill. From Burrough Hill the gentle track route to Burton Lazars, passes the site of the old Leper hospital there. (This walk could be shortened considerably by omitting Burton Lazars, and making it a Little Dalby to Burrough Hill circuit, of 4 miles, using a mile of country road to Little Dalby.)

Burrough Hill Iron Age fort stands on the edge of an escarpment 1½ miles from Somerby and 1 mile from

the village of Burrough on the Hill and 2 miles from Great Dalby. There is a good car park with toilets and picnic area. The main drive leads from the car park directly to the main entrance through the ramparts. The hill is a spectacular flat plateau encircled by a high rampart. The toposcope in one corner gives details of views which can be seen from the high and windy hill. The woods below are open for access and make a marvellous picnic spot.

From Burrough Hill to Burton Lazars (4 miles) From the toposcope inside the fort walk with the ramparts on your left (due north, towards Lincoln cathedral!). Just to the right of the corner ahead of you a gap in the ramparts forms a gateway. A steep descent here, close to the wooden fencing on your left, brings you to a path which goes parallel with the ramparts but at a lower level. (*Beyond this on the other side of the steep valley lies the Dalby Hills path which leads to Little Dalby*).

Do not descend to the bottom of the valley but turn left at the end of the wood to pass through the two farm gates. Walk close to the wood on your left.

Note the green lane straight ahead of you, beyond the next field. This is your route to Burton Lazars. (To reach the green lane, you should walk close to the main body of the wood and then follow a hedge on your left until you reach the road, where you need to turn right. But do not worry if you find yourself walking on a well trodden path leading you down close to a hedge and stream on your right to reach the road. Simply turn left along the road to reach the green lane.)

Go through the gate which leads into the green lane. Initially this is a wide track between hedges. Even when the hedges diappear, the track is perfectly obvious and for the next mile you can feel free to enjoy the views and converse with any companions. When the lane meets the Great Dalby-Little Dalby road, turn right.

(If you wish to take the short cut continue along this road and follow the instructions from Little Dalby.)

To continue to Burton Lazars turn left after a few yards along the road, to continue northwards along Sandy Lane, a similarly beautiful green track.

Walk uphill with the hedge on your right, turning round at intervals to admire the views of Burrough Hill. *The views from the top of this Gartree Hill are spectacular, with Burrough Hill behind you and the Melton Mowbray valley ahead.* Continue downhill. You need to turn right just before the end of the wide double hedging. This leads to a derelict farm and workshops. Turn left opposite the house and go through the wide gap in the hedge. Keep up on the high ground and walk straight towards Burton Lazars Hall in the trees ahead. (In the first field you will be walking parallel with Sandy Lane on your left and then parallel with a hedge below you on your right.)

You should meet a corner of a field and then walk with the hedge on your right. Meet the field track which comes from Sandy Lane. Continue close to the hedge on your right. Pass Burton Lazars Hall and continue across the field where the foundations of the 15th century hospital and church once stood. Make your way to the bottom right corner of this long field and join the drive which goes in front of the big Georgian three storey farmhouse. Pass Pepper's farm on your left and continue down to the busy Melton Road (A606) and the centre of Burton Lazars.

Burton Lazars, though an ancient settlement, has few modern facilities, and I'm afraid you can't rely on a friendly refreshment provided for you here. You are, however, only one and a half miles from Melton Mowbray, where there are shops, cafes, pubs and hotels.

Melton Mowbray lies one and a half miles to your left and the start of the footpath to Burrough lies downhill to your right. (A short stretch of busy road. Take care!)

Walk 21 – Burrough Hill

From Burton Lazars to Burrough Hill. (4 ½ miles)

From Burton Lazars walk along the A606 Melton Road, away from Melton and towards Langham and Oakham. Pass Lime Street on your right and a footpath sign on your left and continue downhill for one field, past Burton parkland on your right. Turn right at the gate which brings you into the corner of the field. Look for Little Dalby church spire on the hill ahead. This is your marker.
(A word of warning at this point! The next three fields are usually badly obstructed with crops (a feature of the whole Melton area! Complaints should be addressed to the LCC footpath department and not to the author! But the rest of the walk is so beautiful that it is worth persevering over this stretch.)
Keeping in line with the church, cross the field, moving away from the road on your left. The crossing point is about halfway along the hedge which leads to the road. There is a double concrete plank footbridge across the ditch, between two trees.

Cross the next field with the church spire slightly to your right to reach the crossing which is about a hundred yards from the trees along the stream on your left. There is a slim concrete plank bridge over the ditch, which leads you into a field with a conifer plantation over to your left and a hedge over to your right.
If the crops are high or obviously sprayed with chemicals, keep close to the stream on your left. Pass the plantation of conifer trees, with a bald patch in the centre which local farmers tell you is the site of the 15th century leper cemetery where corpses were buried in quicklime and where nothing now will grow. (The map tells a less colourful story. You are walking near the site of the moated Grange, with a stream on your left.)
In the corner of the field is a pheasantry in the conifer plantation. Your crossing point is 200 yards to the right of it, where there is a good cartbridge to the left of a hawthorn tree.
Keep making for the church spire.

The crossing is in the corner of the field, near the stream spinney.
(There is a proper gap crossing just to the right of the stream corner.)
Cut across the corner of the field to meet the stream on your left and cross the cart bridge. Turn right for a few yards along a well kept path.
(This headland path actually leads you to the road, where you can turn left to walk into Little Dalby.
To follow the definitive footpath you need to go through the handgate beside the farm gate on your left (in line with the church spire). Pass a mound on your right and walk across the field parallel with the hedge on your left.
Go through the farm gate (aiming for the left of the church spire) and swing left, making for the red brick deserted looking house at the left of the farm.
Go through a farm stackyard (often obstructed by farm machinery) keeping close to the hedge on your left and go through the gap on your left. Turn right and walk along the little lane to the left of the farm. This brings you out on the road opposite

the lane which leads up to Little Dalby church. Turn up the lane which leads to the church. The footpath sign to Somerby is on your left.
But before you leave the village of Little Dalby, visit the beautiful church, which is an absolute "must" on this walk.
When you have fully admired the church and churchyard and the views, return to the houses at the foot of the hill, where the footpath to Somerby is signposted.
Go uphill, over the stile near the corner of the house on your right. Follow the power lines over the crest of the hill, where you can see the church on your right, and descend to cross the drive which leads to the hall. Swing slightly right, to walk parallel with the spinney on your right and the road in the valley on your left.
Cross the drive which leads to the farmhouses on your right and cross into the next field by the footpath sign, to Somerby. The path goes between two spinneys. Pass the one on your left and make for the corner

of the field just before the one on your right. Turn left to cross the footbridge and continue uphill, moving to your right to reach the field track which leads you uphill to Buttermilk Hill spinney.
(The footpath to Somerby lies straight ahead but you need to turn right to reach Burrough Hill.)
Turn right after going through the gate at the end of the field and pass the spinney on your left, moving slightly uphill. Proceed along the well-signposted Dalby Hills path. The path moves very gradually uphill, keeping just below the escarpment. You have time to admire the beautiful views over to your right, where you can see Little Dalby, Burton Lazars and the Church tower of Melton Mowbray. Keep to the high ground and, when the path swings left, you will come to Burrough Hill rising ahead of you. Pass through the fence enclosure. The waymarked path takes you on a left tack up the hill, on a gentle approach to the ramparts and the main front entrance to the fort.

Walk 22 – Burrough Hill

BURROUGH HILL • SOMERBY • BURROUGH ON THE HILL (5½ miles)

The entrance to Burrough Hill lies on a bend in the road half way between Somerby and the village of Burrough on the Hill.

From Burrough Hill Iron Age Fort entrance gate and information board continue along the main track towards the gap in the ramparts. There are marvellous views to your left from this point.
(The first mile of this walk covers the same ground as walk 21, but in the opposite direction.)
Pass through the ramparts (just to the left of the trig. post) into the great flat area of the encampment. We are going to leave the fort through a gap in the far right corner of the "square" but a detour to the toposcope in the left hand corner is a must! The views from this point are spectacular! You can spend time imagining yourself an ancient Briton, defying the Romans or a 17th century racegoer...

From Burrough Hill toposcope continue walking with the rampart on your left until you come to the exit 'gateway' just to the right of the corner, beside a large tree.
Here it is possible to look down the steep slope, past the woodland on your left, flanked by a line of wooden fencing, to a gorsey hill across the valley.
Halfway up the fencing on your left there is a wooden enclosure with a waymark sign. If you look past the fencing you should see a further line of waymark posts, which indicate your route along the Dalby Hills path.
Go through the enclosure and follow the waymark signs.
The grassy track is very beautiful and there is an abundance of wild flowers and butterflies and a fine variety of young trees.
The path is not marked on Ordnance Survey maps, but it goes along the escarpment parallel with the Little Dalby road in the valley on your left. It descends very gradually, finally reaching a wood where it swings right.

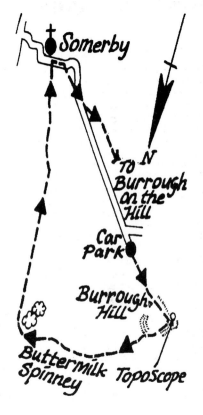

Continue on the waymarked path, for about a mile. At this point the path meets the little Buttermilk Spinney, where the path meets the route from Little Dalby to Somerby. You need to follow the path round to the right, passing through the spinney, close to a fenced off conifer plantation on your right. Emerge into an open area and follow the wide waymarked path with wire fencing on each side.

Our route continues in the same direction to climb the hill ahead, whereas the Dalby path turns left to follow the valley.

We now follow the Leicestershire Round waymark signs all the way into Somerby. The route goes right up to the top of the Punch Bowl hill in front of you.

The crossing point is at the top of the hill just to the left of some scrubby gorse, where a bit of fence can be seen, to the left of a tree.

From the top of the hill you have lovely views back over Little Dalby hall, to the church spire behind it. Grantham mast can also be seen.

Once over the fence you can see the tower of Pickwell church on your left in front of you and the spire of Somerby church ahead. Make towards Somerby spire, which is due south of you.

Cross the field diagonally and you will find yourself walking with a hedge on your right about 200 yards away. Your next crossing is between two ash trees. There is a double footplank here. Continue in the same direction. The hedge is some way over to your right and takes a curving line to the top of the hill. You should make directly for the end of the hedge at the top of the hill. Walk with the hedge on your right. When the field opens up on your right, (with a barn in the top hedge) continue in the same direction, towards a spinney.

The next rough meadow is usually full of lady smock, marsh marigolds, ladies bedstraw, trefoil, meadowsweet and other lovely wild flowers in season. You need to cross the slightly boggy valley and may need to avoid the steepest part by moving right and then left to

regain the line of path.

You need to make for the waymarked stile in the opposite hedge, beyond the spinney area (ignoring the handgate into the field on your left) and in the next field walk with the hedge on your left. The next crossing is just to the right of the field corner. Cross down through a little enclosure to a waymarked stile which brings you out to walk with the hedge on your left. Cross the track which leads to the little Severn Trent water plant (over to your left) and go through a little enclosure. In the next field a line of trees is your marker. Walk with these on your left and go through the narrow neck of the field which leads into a jitty which takes you into the main street of Somerby, opposite Manor Lane.

Somerby to Burrough on the Hill and Burrough Hill. *(2 miles)*

Turn right along Main Street. There are shops in the village and two pubs which provide meals. Pass the Stilton Cheese pub on your left and meet a little private road on your right, called The Field. Turn right and walk along The Field, to cut off a dangerous corner of road with no pavement. Turn right at the junction with the main road and walk for a few yards to a gate in the corner of the first field on your left. (No footpath sign here, but a notice saying 'No Horses'!)

You now have to cross a large ploughed field. You need to keep in the same direction as The Field road, going diagonally right across the field. (Set your sights on the left hand edge of the wood ahead of you and you should reach the corner of the field where the fence meets the hedge on your right.)

Go over the gate in the corner of the field and admire the views over the old gravel pits ahead of you. Turn right and walk with the hedge on your right along the high ground, passing the interesting weird little hummocks of the gravel pit on your left. Pass Burrough Hill House over to your right.

You need to go through one gate and continue walking with the hedge on your right. As you swing further left the spire of Burrough on the Hill village church comes into view.

The hedge you are following swings round the contour of the hill and then bends sharply right, ending at an enclosure of gates. Burrough church spire is straight ahead of you.

Walk downhill with the hedge and isolated trees still on your right. Cross a grassy track which leads to the ruins of a little brick house on your left and go over the fence ahead of you.

Continue down the steep hill, moving slightly away from the hedge on your right. In the bottom left corner of the field there is a flimsy plank bridge over the stream. You need to cross a rather boggy patch of grass to reach it. Make your way up the hill passing to the left of an isolated telegraph pole to reach the top left corner of the field. A stile here, close to a telegraph pole, leads into a narrow jitty between houses. Emerge on the main road in Burrough at the footpath sign. The church is to your left. There is no cafe in the village now, but there is a very pleasant and helpful post office and

general store, near the church. Our walk continues to your right.

It is possible to walk along the road from Burrough on the Hill to Burrough Hill. The entrance is only a mile along the road to Somerby. But for the more adventurous there is an infinitely preferable route which takes you down a green lane and along an old County Road to meet a second County Road which leads you up a steep grassy track passing the ramparts of the iron age hill fort on your left.

From Burrough on the Hill church to Burrough Hill. To follow the green lane route, walk along the road towards Burrough Hill and Somerby. At the end of the village you need to turn left into a lane opposite the old school house, just before the derestriction sign. Go through the handgate beside the farm gate on your right and walk down the green lane, with hedges on each side. This takes you gradually downhill with fine views of Burrough Hill over to your right.

Walk 22 – Burrough Hill

When the double hedge ends, continue in the same direction to reach the bottom hedge, then move right until you reach the corner of the field.

Swing left, through a gap, and walk with the hedge on your right for about 30 yards. Turn right, cross the ditch and go through an old gate. (You might need to search in the undergrowth for it.)

You are now on a County Road, not marked on O.S. maps and because not many people know of its existence and because it has, shamefully, not been waymarked and signposted it is not as well trodden as it deserves to be).

Cross the field and go through the wide gateway opposite (just left of a big ash tree).

Turn left for about 30 yards and then turn right, to continue in the same direction to a gap in the hedge ahead. You are moving towards the left of the foot of Burrough Hill. The toposcope can now be seen above you.

Your next crossing point is to the right of three ash trees. Continue in the same direction until you meet,

just beyond a circular tree-lined pond, the next County Road. Turn right and follow this field road all the way up to the top of Burrough Hill. (It is waymarked as part of the Leicestershire Round.) Pass the toposcope high up on your left. The main entrance to the fort is on your left. This is a good place to stop and look back over the route you have just walked. The information board and the drive to the car park and the toilets and picnic area are straight ahead of you.

Medbourne

Step 11 • Medbourne to Uppingham

Medbourne (Old English Maed burna, a meadow stream) a beautiful little town in the Welland valley, snuggling into the Slawston hill ridge near the Northampton border six miles north east of Market Harborough.

Its pleasing mixture of ironstone and red brick buildings indicate the mixture of soils in the area. The low towered church is of soft mellow ironstone and Hoskins includes it in his list of most interesting Leicestershire churches. It is very picturesquely placed in the centre of the village, (Millward says that its circular enclosure suggests a pre-historic henge or stone circle). The little river Medbourne flows close by.

The main road crosses the stream through a water splash ford beside a narrow medieval pack horse bridge. And there is a most attractive river walk between church and pub. (The Neville Arms, prettily set beside the river and provided with a charming footbridge, is welcoming to walkers.)

Each Easter the village competes with neighbouring Hallaton in the famous Bottle Kicking ceremony.

The town was once a Roman settlement and the site of a Roman villa remains in the field due west of the church. Coins, medals and a tessellated pavement were discovered in 1721. The site is close to the Via Devana (the Gartree Road) which goes through Leicester.

Neville Holt a beautiful unspoilt hamlet near Medbourne, quite off the beaten track. The church is an integral part of the lovely long low buildings of the hall. The south front is described in Transactions of the Leics Archaelogical Soc vol XIII. It contains a good deal of Tudor building. The gem of the building is Thomas Palmer's oriel 1476. The porch was built by Sir Thomas Neville at his own expense in 1635.

The village was in 1728 briefly a spa, advertising its medicinal waters 'efficacious in all acute feverish and inflammatory diseases ....' (Dr Short's pamphlet, quoted by J.B.Firth). The buildings were bought as a prep school on the death of Mr Cosmo Nevill Peake. Neville family monuments are in the church.

The lovely chestnut and lime avenue leading to the village has recently been replanted (Dec 1988) by the Woodland Trust with 96 new saplings of lime and oak.

Blaston (Bleath's tun) a delightful little hamlet with interesting ruins of an old church in parkland by the river and an isolated little church in a meadow. Col. Pen Lloyd (*Anecdotes of Bygone Leicestershire*) accounts for the origin of the two chapels in Blaston, both built by King Richard about 1190. He relates the traditional story of King Richard's lover whom he housed in his hunting box at Blaston and for whom he built two chapels, so that he could move her across from one to another whenever he had trouble with the bishop! Blaston stands on the border of land belonging to the sees of Peterborough and of Lincoln.

Before 1840 there was another road which ran behind Blaston Hall parallel with the street but higher up the slope.

This was part of the main highway between Hallaton and Uppingham, but there is evidence it was not passable for carriages which could only enter and leave Blaston by the Hallaton end. The Lord of the Manor, the Rev. G. Fenwicke (d.1863), suggested it be closed and the town street extended to form the main highway.

Blaston Hall (demolished c.1930) stood on the north side of the road near the west end of the village. It was built by the Rev. John Owsley (d.1835) who was Lord of the Manor, Rector and patron of Blaston for 68 years. Alterations were made by Thomas Hardcastle in late 19th century. His son T.A.Hardcastle was the last to occupy the house before it was demolished. All that remains are the late-18th century gate piers of two entrance drives, a brick stable (also contemporary with the house) and a detached billiard room (probably built by Thomas Hardcastle).

The so-called Manor House is a former farmhouse to which additions were made in the 19th century to provide a residence for the Fenwicke family. It was divided into three separate dwellings c.1950.

Crane's Cottages (tablet 1647 restored 1907 TAH) in the early 19th century was the Chamberlayne Arms public house.

Thatch House, newly renovated, is dated 1617, restored 1907 T.A.H.

Stone House is sometimes open to the public for charity. In its gardens is a fine collection of stone chinoiserie. The Stone House was occupied after 1919 by Mrs Fernie, daughter of Hardcastle of Blaston hall, who became Master of the Fernie Hunt in 1919 when her husband died, and from 1937 by Col.P.H.Lloyd, also Master of the Hunt.

Sir Malcolm Sargent, the conductor, once lived in the village.

Horninghold Before the Norman Conquest the manor of Horninghold was held by four thegns, Osuld, Osmund, Roulf and Levrick. After the Conquest it passed to Robert, lord of Belvoir. It later became crown propery and was in 1553 sold to Sir William Turpin of Knaptoft whose manor house, much restored, still stands between the green and the church. The church has an early 12th century south doorway.

The rest of the village is a re-creation by the Hardcastles of Blaston Hall. Thomas Hardcastle (died 1902) bought the manor in 1880 and his son T.A.Hardcastle rebuilt a 'model village', planted with a great variety of trees and ornamental shrubs. To the west of the village is a fine 18th century avenue of lime trees. The large red brick stables are of 1882, and were once used for 30 hunters.

Most of the village renovation is dated 1905-1911. The cottages are built of local ironstone, set in spacious gardens. The former Globe Inn became two cottages, with a tablet, dated 1911, recording the fact. T.A.Hardcastle sold the estate in 1916 and died in 1941.

In 1911 the population was 124. Now as you walk through the village it seems a ghost town, with no shop, no children, no school, no pub. But it wins prizes for being the Best Kept Village!

Stockerston *(Old English, Stoccfaesten tun, a stronghold built of tree trunks).*
The Hall c. 1800 stands on the site of an older house, next to the church of St Peter (13th century, ironstone and limestone). The church has a good deal of 15th century glass and Philip Ennis (Rutland Border Rides, vol V) mentions leaded glass windows on which apprentices have etched their names, such as 'Francis Tyke, Plumber 1757'. There is also a collection of finely carved medieval bench ends in the church.
In 1832 it is reported there were no schools in the village. In 1833 there was a Sunday school for 8-10 children. In 1888 there was an infants school but there has never been a school for older children. The last time I saw a child in Stockerston, a couple of years ago, he told me he was the only child in the village and went to school by bus.

Uppingham, the ham of the Uppingas, the people on the hill, an Early English settlement about 500 A.D. and now a pleasant little market town. The market was first granted by Edward 1 in 1281. The church, attractively positioned at the back of the market square is on an ancient site, but the building itself has been heavily restored. Uppingham school, founded 1584 by Robert Johnson, (who also founded Oakham school) the son of a prosperous Stamford wool merchant and later archdeacon of Leicester. The original small school house still stands near the churchyard. The famous headmaster Thring was appointed in 1853 when there were 23 boarders. The school expanded and now dominates the life of the town. The main buildings are of 1863-5.

CELIA FIENNES Journeys travelling in 1682-1712 (Through Peterborough and Leicester to Wolseley) describes her route through Uppingham:
From Wanstead to Duddington (and passed over a very good stone bridge). Here we are near the quarrys of stone and all the houses and walls are built of stone, as in Gloucestershire: this river and bridge enter'd me into Leicestershire which is a very rich country, red land, good corne of all sorts and grass both fields and enclosures; you see a good way upon their hills the bottoms full of enclosure woods and different sorts of manureing and herbage, amongst which are placed many little towns, which gives great pleasure for the traveller to view;
the miles are long but hitherto pretty hard good way (she was travelling on horseback) to Coppingham (Uppingham) 5 mile more, which is a neat Market town; Saturday is their market which is very good affording great quantitys of corn leather yarne and cattle, such a concourse of people that my Landlord told me he used to have 100 horse set up at his inn and there were many publick houses here: you see here very large fine sheep and very good land but very deep bad roads; from hence to Leicester which they call but 13 mile but the longest 16 I ever went and the most tiresome, being full of sloughs, clay deep way, that I was near 11 hours going but 25 mile, as they reckon it, between Wansford and Leicester town. (They were using the old local Long Mile. It is 33 statute miles.) A footman could have gone much faster than I could ride.

Lyddington 2 miles from Uppingham, (written as Lideton in Domesday Book, 1086 (tun on River Hlyde). An Anglo-Saxon settlement founded during the 5th-7th centuries, it was given to the See of Lincoln after the Conquest. In the reign of King John (1199-1216) the Bishop of Lincoln had a house and grounds in the village. The Bedehouse is well worth a visit and the museum notices give fascinating history of the great fishponds, which were marvels of engineering, enabling the fish to be farmed.

Stoke Dry A tiny place, with only a couple of farms and houses. The little church is most interesting. It has a porch and upper room and impressive monuments to the Digby family (of Tilton). The Gunpowder Plot Digby is mourned on his tomb by his father. *Legend has it that a tunnel runs from Stoke Dry to Neville Holt.*

The Eyebrook Reservoir was constructed in 1935 as a water supply for Corby steel works. The river Eyebrook was dammed to produce the 44 acre sheet of water, which was opened in 1940. In 1943 it was used by the Dambusters (617 Squadron) flying Lancasters from RAF Scamton to perfect their technique... (Poor old Rutland always seems to be used for low-flying aircraft to practise the Defense of the Realm!)

Step 11 • Medbourne to Uppingham

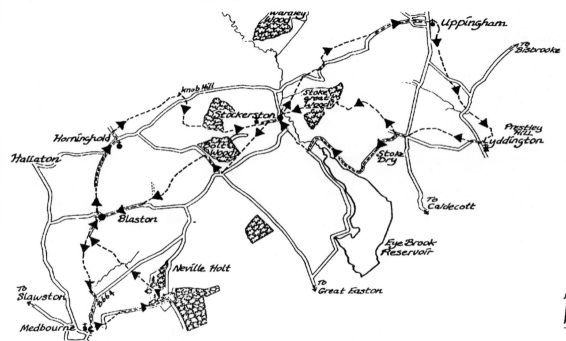

Walk 23 – Medbourne to Uppingham

MEDBOURNE · NEVILLE HOLT · BLASTON

4 miles along mainly track and tree lined driveway with one mile of cross country hilly farmland and a short detour through parkland to see the quiet and secret hamlet of Neville Holt.

Medbourne lies to the north west of Market Harborough and south west of Uppingham on the B664 road.

From Medbourne Church on the main B664 road (Uppingham - Market Harborough) walk along Rectory Lane which is just opposite the church. At the end of this very pretty walled lane a kissing gate leads you along a causeway across the green track of the old disused railway to a kissing gate at the other side. Follow the tarmac strip to the gate in the next little field and cross the road which comes from Medbourne to Neville Holt. Go up the field ahead of you, moving quite steeply uphill, parallel with power lines. Pass the corner of a house garden on your left. Go through the gateway ahead, and swing right. Go through a bridle gate in the wall ahead and pass the house on your right. Cross the drive and make your way to the far left corner of the field, where you will find an interesting old slab stone crossing set in the wall. Turn right and walk along the road to Neville Holt. This becomes a lovely tree lined drive, passing through wrought iron gates with posts surmounted by crowns and bulls' heads (the heraldic device of the Nevilles). Pass a gate house on your left and continue on the drive to the T-junction.

The continuation of our walk is to our left, but it would be a shame to miss the best views of Neville Holt so we are going to make a small detour through the hamlet. Turn right and walk along the road to the wrought iron gates. Turn left and walk along the drive (the discouraging notices do not apply to the use of the footpath. Do not be deterred. It is a right of way.) Pass the front of the magnificent house and chapel on your left. Pass

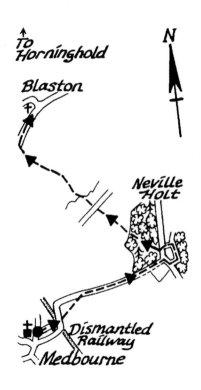

Walk 23 – Medbourne to Uppingham

the stable arch and turn left. Walk through the small gate beside the stable block building and walk along the gravel drive to the footpath sign. You now join the main village street through this tiny secluded and beautifully kept Elizabethan hamlet, with walled gardens and stone cottages. Turn left to follow the tall garden wall to meet the road, just past the telephone box.

Cross the road to the bridleway sign and go over the stile. Walk diagonally right across this big pasture field to the bridle gate in the far right corner, where the hedge and fence meet.

The village straight ahead of you is Hallaton. Blaston, your next goal, lies out of sight in the valley between you and Hallaton.

At the other side of the bridle gate you come to a field corner with a hedge ahead of you leading directly towards Hallaton. Walk with this hedge on your left.

As you descend the hill note the marker hedge on the opposite side of the road, leading straight up to a square spinney at the top of the hill.

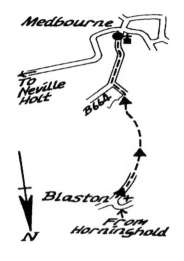

You need to cross the road and walk uphill with this hedge on your right. To get there, you have to cross a stretch of ploughed field beyond the road and cross the bridge over the stream about 1( ) yards to the right of the marker hedge. Once across the stream, swing left to cross to the far side of

the hedge. Turn right and follow this hedge uphill for one field, towards the square spinney, and then swing diagonally left.

Aim for an isolated tree on the skyline in the far left corner of the field. A gap to the right of the tree brings you out to meet a hedge on your right.

The hills you have just crossed are rather bleak but the views ahead of you are very attractive. The lovely village of Hallaton is on the hillside. Walk downhill with the hedge on your right to the Blaston-Medbourne field road.

At this point you can decide whether to continue the walk to Horninghold or to return to Medbourne. Your route back to Medbourne goes left along this field road for a gentle $1\frac{1}{2}$ mile stroll but before you go you should turn right to see Blaston village with its little church and its lovely stone houses set in beautiful parkland and its deserted church down by the river.

BLASTON · HORNINGHOLD · STOCKERSTON · BLASTON · 7 miles

(A mile of field road followed by a rather heavy stretch of arable land from Horninghold to Knob Hill. This can be avoided by a mile of road walking, if you prefer it. The walk to Stockerston is across pasture land, with beautiful views over to the Eyebrook reservoir. The descent into Stockerston and the climb up again can be avoided if you wish to shorten the walk by 2 miles. But if you do go down to the village, you can add on the short trip to the reservoir, which adds on mile in each direction. The return to Blaston is mainly downhill.)

From Blaston church walk away from the village along the Hallaton-Stockerston road for 50 yards. When the road bends left, take the gated road on your right to Horninghold and walk up along the avenue of trees for three quarters of a mile. *This is a lovely avenue, with fine views. Hallaton can be seen over to your left in front of you.*

When you reach the road, turn right and walk into the village of *Horninghold*, a very pretty village where every house looks like a stately manor house and every garden is properly manicured. Turn left when you reach the church and walk down the dead end road. (On your left a house bears a sign to indicate that The Old Globe Inn stood here and the house was restored by TAH 1903, as were so many houses in the village.)

Pass the (well hidden) telephone box on your left and turn right to walk along the drive beside two cottages (one is the old post office) and continue through the avenue of horse chestnut trees. (The entrance is beside the gate marked Private Entrance and the crossing point is usually obstructed. I cross the metal railings into the field on the left and walk with the avenue of trees on my right.) There is an old gateway (usually obstructed) at the end of the avenue.

Continue with the hedge on your right. Keep in the same direction

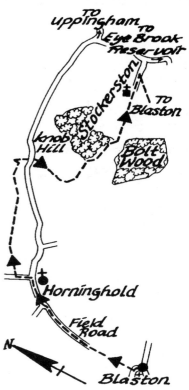

and cross the hedge in front of you. You are now going to continue in this direction keeping on the highest ground and moving along the crest of the hill, parallel with the road, to reach Muckelborough Farm.

In the first field you walk uphill and pass to the left of a tree lined pond. In the second field there is also a pond on your right, right at the top of the hill but this is more difficult to see, especially when crops are high. In the third field the red roof of Muckelborough Farm comes into view and Knob Hill Farm can be seen to the right of it, on the opposite side of the road. Aim for Muckelborough Farm.

In the last field you should make for the left of the farm gate. There is a flimsy fence crossing to the left of a tall ash tree. The grassy track of Allexton Lane, an old field road, comes in on your left from Allexton and meets the road here at Knob Hill. Turn right and join the track, passing Muckelborough Farm on your right.

Cross the Knob Hill Road and go through the gate to the left of Knob Hill farm. Walk through the farm-yard to the gate at the far side. The track is not clearly visible on the ground though it was once the main Allexton-Stockerston lane.

Walk uphill and pass under the telegraph wires until you are walking close to the hedge on your right. A gate in the bottom right corner of the field leads you onto the bridleway from Horninghold to Stockerston, where you need to turn left to descend to Stockerston.

(If, however, you wish to shorten the walk and omit the descent to and climb from the village, you can omit the next eight paragraphs and continue with the hedge on your right, keeping to the high ground until you meet the road, at the footpath sign. Turn left and walk along the road to reach the footpath sign (about 200 yards away). Turn right here and walk the route described on page 132*)

Turn left and follow the hedge on your left. Move right to pass the little corner which juts out and continue downhill with the hedge on your left. The ground descends quite sharply and there are fine views over to Stoke Dry woods and to the Eyebrook reservoir beyond.

When the hedge ends, continue in the same direction across the small piece of open ground and walk with the wood on your left. There is a gate in the far neck of the field. This leads you into a field with a fence on your right. There is usually a good headland track here, which you follow. The lovely trees of Stockerston Hall come into view and you pass close to the elegant hall and garden, on your left, next to the little church of *Stockerston*. Go through the signposted bridlegate and turn right along the avenue of lime trees (Church Lane) which leads into the tiny hamlet of Stockerston. (If you wish to extend the walk a little you can go down the lane and turn right at the cottages for a half mile walk to the Eyebrook reservoir, returning to this point to continue the walk back to Blaston and Medbourne, where you started.)

(For a longer walk you can add on the Stockerston to Uppingham loop at this point..... or you can save that for another day!)

To return to Blaston from Stockerston walk halfway along Church Lane (the lime tree avenue between the church and the cottages on Uppingham Road, Stockerston). Here a footpath sign points you back into the field you have just come from.

You are now going to move away from Stockerston and go diagonally across this field through a series of waymarked stiles to reach the top of the hill between two woods on the skyline. As you climb up the hill you will see a gate close to Bolt wood on your right.

Continue in the same direction, walking close to the wood on your right. Go through the parish boundary hedge ahead of you. (There is a waymarked stile hidden in the hedge to the right of some old corrugated iron sheds.)

Keeping in the same direction make for the cross roads signposts and the triangulation marker in the far corner of the field. (Medbourne 3 Uppingham 4 Horninghold $1\frac{1}{4}$)

Turn right and walk along the Stockerston Lane road towards Hallaton and Horninghold for about a

Field Road to Medbourne

Blaston

Blaston Lodge

Highlands Spinney

To Great Easton

Bolt Wood

From Knob Hill

Stockerston

To Uppingham

N

quarter of a mile. Turn left at the bridleway sign to return to Blaston.

*From the bridleway sign, walk with the hedge on your right for two fields to reach Highland Spinney. Keep in the same direction and go through the gate which brings you out to the right of the spinney. Walk with the spinney on your left.

Blaston is now in the valley downhill ahead of you to your right. As you descend the hill, passing Blaston Lodge farm, over to your right, you can see, if you look carefully, a curve of the lane you are going to join to take you into Blaston. This lane goes between the woods and a circular treelined pond.

To reach this curve in the lane you need to move away from the wood and cross the fields on your right. You need to turn right at a point where there is a slight bend in the hedge on your left. (You may see the remains of an old gatepost and a dead tree!)

(The farmer has recently taken to

leaving a wide mown headland right round this field, and you might prefer to follow this strip round three sides of the field to reach the crossing point between wood and hawthorn hedge. The choice is yours!.)

Aim for a gap between the wood on your left and a hawthorn hedge. Cross the cart bridge and continue uphill in the same direction to cross the next field, making for the trees on the skyline marking the end of the wood on your left.

You should reach the farm drive where it curves and passes the tree lined pond on your right. This takes you to the road into Blaston. Turn right and walk through the village of Blaston.

From Blaston to Medbourne

To return to Medbourne turn left at the road junction, passing Blaston church on your right, and follow the field road 1½ miles to meet the road. Turn right and cross over the railway bridge (take care here! There is no pavement!) and into the town of Medbourne.

**STOCKERSTON •
UPPINGHAM • LYDDINGTON •
STOKE DRY • STOCKERSTON
$7\frac{1}{2}$ miles.**

Uphill to Uppingham, downhill
thereafter! For the final stretch you
have a choice of a road walk beside
the Eyebrook reservoir to see the
water birds or a high pasture walk
along an old green lane followed by
a walk through the woods to
descend to Stockerston.

From Stockerston village, opposite
the lane to the church, a footpath
sign points the way along a path at
the left of a terrace of stone
cottages. At the end of the garden
the path goes slightly left across an
open field to a foot bridge, just to
the left of the cart bridge.
Continue in the same direction to
cross the next field, walking with a
hedge over to your right (and the
stream over to your left). A gate at
the end of the field takes you into a
rough little fenced off corner of the
next field with a farm shed.
Pass the farm shed and walk with

the hedge on your left. (The true
line of path should go slightly
right, uphill to cross a stream
gulley just below a tongue of
woodland but the crossing is
obstructed and difficult to find.)
At the end of the field cross
through the bridle gate ahead
(ignoring the gate on your left)
and turn right, walking for 100
yards uphill until the stream gulley
on your right widens up. (This is
where the true crossing should
come.)
You now need to make your way
diagonally left across the field,
making for a hill surmounted by a
clump of trees. (This is your next
goal.) As you cross the field you
will see the Dangerous Bend sign
on the road. Make for this and
emerge on the road at the gate in
the corner of the field. (If the way
is obstructed by crops you could
continue up beside the wood and
then turn left at the end of the field
to reach this point.)
Turn right and walk uphill along
the main Stockerston-Uppingham
road for 100 yards. The road now

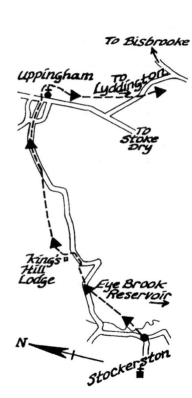

makes a hairpin bend to the right but the footpath goes through a gate on your left and then straight up the hill to the tall clump of trees on the skyline. There is a gate at the right of the clump of trees which leads onto the road again.

Turn left and walk along the road towards Uppingham for 200 yards, passing the house and the drive to Kings Hill Lodge on your left. Turn left at the farm drive and then turn right to walk with the fence on your left and the hedge on your right, following the waymarked route. After 300 yards, at a point where the ground begins to drop down quite sharply, you can see over Wardley Wood to the Uppingham A47 road on the horizon. Here you need to cross the hedge on your right (near a holly bush).

The next field is a long narrow one, with houses on the road to your right. Cross slightly left, to a junction of hedges opposite and cross into the corner of the next field, close to a hedge on your right. You now continue in this direction, crossing a series of small fields going from the corner of fields to a point midway along the hedge on your left. You are heading for the church spires of Uppingham. The route is at the moment well waymarked and there are footplanks and double fences with stiles at each crossing point. The last crossing place is through a gap in the hedge. The footpath rejoins the road at a footpath sign by a gate at a bend in the road.

Turn left and walk along Stocker-ston Road into *Uppingham*.

The town is a small market town, dominated by the public school and all its works. In the main street lies the Market square, with eating places and public toilets.

At the market square turn right to see Uppingham church. You can turn left just in front of the church and weave your way left along a path which brings you out beside a flight of steps on your right. At the bottom of these steps you will see the footpath sign to Lyddington on the opposite side of the road. (You can reach this point by following Queen Street, passing the library and small car park and continuing down onto South View road.)

From Uppingham to Lyddington,

Follow the signposted footpath to Lyddington, which begins as a little track between hedges, from South View Road, going steeply downhill. A stile at the bottom leads you uphill to a waymarked stile near a telegraph pole. Walk with the hedge on your right and keep in the same direction on a well used track going through an area of rough ground. Keep close to the hedge and fencing on your right. Continue across a small lane. Go downhill, passing a house on your right and cross the footplank bridge. Continue in the same direction, uphill through a small belt of woodland, until you reach the school playing field, with a sports hall on your right. Make your way diagonally left to cross the wooden fence near the far left corner of the field, where a bit of hedge juts out. Continue to the next waymarked stile, which leads you onto an old green lane between hedges. Cross straight over the lane. You can

Walk 25 – Medbourne to Uppingham

now see the spire of Lyddington church, your next goal, ahead of you. Walk down to the bottom left corner of the next, big field to meet the road. The footpath continues in the same direction on the opposite side of the road, past an isolated tree which you can use as a marker. Go over the crest of the hill. Pass the isolated tree and continue to the opposite hedge. Cross the fence and walk downhill in the next field, still aiming for the church spire. You need to cross the hedge on your right about halfway down the field.

Continue downhill in the same direction, to cross the fence in the hedge ahead and go to the far right corner of the next field, to the stile by the footpath sign. This brings you out on the road close to a green lane. Follow the footpath opposite the green lane. The first field has a stream in it which is at first some way away over to your right. Walk straight across the field to meet the hedge and stream and then walk with it on your right.

A series of waymarked stiles through small fields lead you past a lake and

some very lovely ornamental gardens on your right.

As you approach the foot of the smoothly rounded Prestley Hill you meet on your right a lane which takes you into *Lyddington*. Turn right along this lane and then turn left almost immediately and cross the well hidden stile which takes you onto a green lane leading directly to the famous fishponds of Lyddington. Here you need to turn right and follow the hedge on your right until you meet the gravel drive between the lovely stone built houses of this picture book village. *Lyddington village with its famous Bede House deserves a visit.*

From Lyddington to Stoke Dry

From Lyddington village green take the road signposted to Stoke Dry near the White Hart pub. In 200 yards, where the houses end, (just past the derestriction sign) turn right at the footpath sign and make for the top of the hill. Walk parallel with the hedge on your right and go over the highest part of the hill. The stile is in the

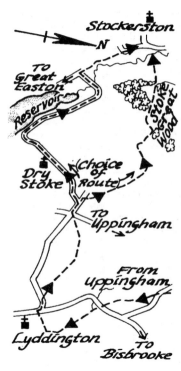

top right corner of the field (although the map marks it down a little to the left, beside the ash tree). Go straight ahead to the next double fence crossing and continue in the same general direction to the next hedge, keeping on the high ground. Go through the bridle gate. The path now swings left (following the telegraph wires) to meet the road at the crossroads.

(Stoke Dry $\frac{1}{2}$ mile Uppingham 2) Take the road to Stoke Dry.

You can if you wish follow this road all the way back to Stockerston. It goes through the little hamlet of Stoke Dry (where you can stop to look in the church and see the upper room where the Gunpowder plot was probably NOT planned) and continue down to the Eyebrook reservoir, walking close to the water's edge on your left, where you can admire the water birds. At the road junction turn right and walk along the road into Stockerston.

The footpath route gives you better views of the whole reservoir and a chance to walk through a wood.

The choice is yours.

The footpath route goes along the road as far as Manor farm and then goes through cattle pens, where it follows a well marked old lane. The hedge is at first only on your left, but in the second field it goes through a section where both hedges remain. Continue along this high ground (with lovely views down over the Eyebrook reservoir). Walk through the wide drift between hedges and then continue walking with a hedge on your right.

When the field ends you need to swing left to reach a gate which leads onto a narrow green bridle path across a scrubby area, with a hedge on your right.

When the fenced off path ends continue with the hedge and an old drystone wall on your right, keeping on high ground. When you reach the wood ahead, the track swings right, still with drystone walling.

Walk with the wood on your left for a short stretch and then turn left through the gate and down the well used straight ride through the woods. You need to follow this track right

through the wood. You come to a cross roads of paths in the centre of the wood. Go straight across and continue downhill, moving slightly left.

The problem now is not to go too far on this track. When you can see that you are near the bottom of the wood and that the path is gradually swinging left you need to go right, along a path which is not easy to find (though a good waymark sign is all that is needed).

This little path soon leads you to a bridle gate at the end of the wood. Continue downhill across the field (halfway between wire fences on each side). Go through the cattle pens and turn left to cross the footbridge you crossed at the beginning of the walk.

Go diagonally left and find the footpath which passes down the right side of the row of cottages on the road. Stockerston church is directly ahead, up Church lane, past the telephone box. (This is the route you need to take if you wish to continue to Blaston and Medbourne.)

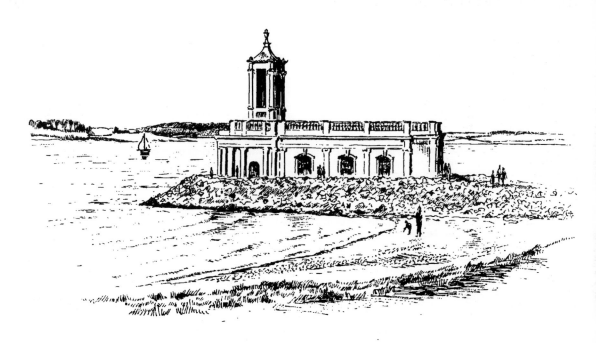

Normanton – Rutland Water

Rutland: *(Rot land, red land?)*
The Royal domain of Roteland was given by Ethelred the Unready as dowry for his Norman queen, Emma, who later married King Canute. The gift was in turn passed on by her son Edward the Confessor to his wife, Edith (whose name is enshrined in that of Edith Weston). It was part of her property in 1066. In 1204 it was given by King John to his queen Isobel (but later he took it back!)
The land was mainly forest, wild rough wooded country. There were very early Anglo Saxon settlements and a large burial ground has been found at Empingham, with skeletons of young men, as though after a large battle. It is still sparsely inhabited and the county is one fifth under water. *It (reluctantly) became part of Leicestershire in 1974.*

Rutland Water originally called Empingham reservoir, was completed in 1976. It is the largest artificial lake in the country. The river Gwash feeds naturally into the reservoir but most of the water is pumped in from the rivers Nene and Welland. It is well stocked with trout and fishing permits can be obtained at Whitwell. The whole reservoir is about 5 miles long and the perimeter 24 miles. The maximum depth is 100 feet. The dam at the Empingham end is nearly a mile long.
The limnological tower gives access to the base of the reservoir and is used for inspections of the water. There are information centres and tourist attractions at Whitwell, Barnsdale and Sykes lane and Normanton and a nature reserve educational centre near Manton.

If you decide to have a tour of the reservoir you will see various small villages with fine churches. The villages of Whitwell, Empingham, Edith Weston, Manton all border the reservoir and all provide refreshment and interest. Egleton has a fine church with a Romanesque elaborately decorated doorway. Whitwell church is mainly Norman. Empingham has a fine 14th century tower and the little church of Normanton, preserved on a peninsula of its own, is a delightful Georgian building, all that is left of the village itself which was depopulated in the 18th century. All of these can be seen across the shores of the lake from our Hambleton peninsula walk.

Hambleton Peninsula The walk requires little introduction and few instructions, for the area is, after all, one of the main beauty spots of Leicestershire and Rutland. Many of us who signed the petitions against drowning the farmland and the villages of Middle and Nether Hambleton now enjoy the beautiful stretch of water which the reservoir provides. Doubtless the concern and the hostility to the very idea of a reservoir which would drown so much of the small county of Rutland influenced the water authorities in their decision to pay attention to the provision of facilities so that the public could enjoy the benefits of this water haven. These facilities included the provision of footpaths to replace those that were drowned. There is no longer a short path to walk from Hambleton to Whitwell or Normanton or Empingham or Edith Weston but there is this perimeter path which gives you fine views of them across the water. (The only missing bit at the moment is the short stretch near the nature reserve at Manton. This, as you will see, affects our walk from Manton to Lyndon.)

Hambleton village is very pleasant and quiet. There is no car park and you will need to park with consideration, so as not to cause obstruction in the village street. The pub has a terrace with a lovely view over the water.
Hambleton Old Hall (down on the water's edge) was 'new erected' in 1611. (The present Hambleton Hall up on the hill, in the main street, is an expensive and exclusive hotel) but has been known to serve afternoon tea to two ladies in rambling gear, discreetly modified by a modest top covering and a quick wash!

Burley House a stately home on the grand scale, re-built 1694-1708 for the Finch family. Recently televised in a series which included Chatsworth. (The interior of the house was also used for episodes of Upstairs, Downstairs.) It stands on the site of earlier houses, where kings and queens were entertained. James I visited Sir John Harington in 1603. George Villiers, first Duke of Buckingham, built a second house "among the noblest seats in England", according to John Evelyn, and gave a banquet for King Charles I in which Jeffrey Hudson the 9" high dwarf child was served up in a cold pie. From our walk we look over the water to the elegant South front of the building, sold to the Finch family when the second Duke of Buckingham died in debt.

Lyndon a small village 4 miles SE of Oakham. Church rather heavily restored. The Hall built 1671-3. Thomas Barker of Lyndon hall married the sister of Gilbert White of Selbourne, who often mentions Lyndon in his writing.
The Top Hall, which we pass in the fields as we approach the village, is c. 1680.

Manton *Maen tun OE town on a rock*
3 miles north of Uppingham. An attractive village with many 17th century houses. The Church of St Mary has a 'curiously haphazard outline' (Hoskins) with a notable early thirteenth century west front, rebuilt at a time of great prosperity, and a distinctively Rutland type of Bell cote.

Normanton The name gives evidence of Norse settlement. Most invaders were Danish but these were Norwegian, hence Northmen's village.
The village was destroyed when Sir Gilbert Heathcote enlarged his deer park 1764. The villagers were removed to Empingham. Sir Gilbert's son pulled down the church in 1764 and built the pretty little white Georgian one which now stands so elegantly preserved on Rutland Water.

Wing *(Scandinavian Vengi, a wide open field)* about 3 miles NE of Uppingham.
Our walk passes close to the medieval maze, around which penitents probably kneeled their way to the centre.

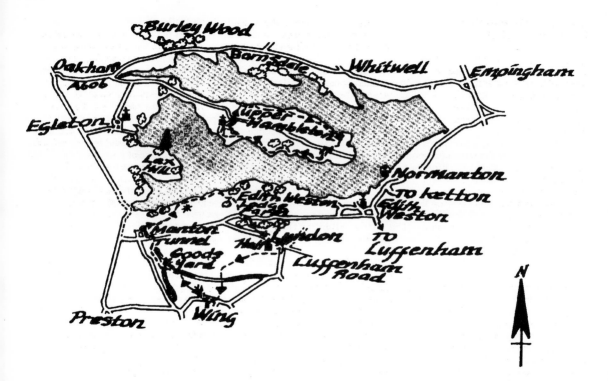

Walk 26 – Rutland Water

HAMBLETON PENINSULA • RUTLAND WATER

A 4 mile stroll on a well marked and surfaced track along the water's edge of Rutland water. Upper Hambleton village is on a No Through road which forks off to the right one mile beyond Oakham on the A606 to Stamford.

From Hambleton village pass the pub on your left and the church on your right. Pass the post office and the Old Vicarage and then turn left (at the footpath sign) through a wooden farm gate which takes you along a grassy track between hedges and through a little belt of beech trees into an open field overlooking the water.

Go downhill to the bottom right corner of this field where you meet the perimeter track as it bends down to meet the water's edge. Follow the hedge on your right.

This track takes you all round the peninsula, enabling you to walk easily, concentrating simply on the lovely and varied views, the wild flowers and the many water birds. As you go round you can look across the water to Barnsdale and Whitwell (with information centres and car parks and toilets and picnic areas). As you proceed you will see the long dam at the end of the reservoir and Empingham Church spire beyond it. You can go to the water's edge and hear the water lapping and look across to see the fields which have been cut diagonally by the reservoir.

As you round the end of the peninsula you can see on the far shore the lovely little Georgian church of Normanton which was saved from the flooding by being buttressed upon its own little peninsula.

You cross the road (now gated and closed to traffic) which forms the 'spine' of the peninsula and which used to lead into Edith Weston and Normanton. You can walk down to the end of this road and see where it now takes a nose dive into the water.

Continue on the track to complete your walk along the other side of the peninsula.

Across the water you can see Edith Weston and the sails of the many yachts of the large sailing club. There is always some activity to see on the water. In one bay there will be quiet fishermen and swans and in another surfboarders and yachts. You will meet occasional cyclists or fishermen's cars on the track but you won't find much to disturb the peace of this little oasis of land.

After you have passed through a lovely large wooded area you will see ahead of you Hambleton Old Hall standing very grandly on its own peninsula and as you approach the drive to the house there is a stile on your right.

This takes you up a steep hill in a field with a house on your left. The stile in the top of the field is halfway along the top hedge and you emerge with a wood on your right.

Continue in the same direction to the bridle gate beside the farm gate which leads you via a grassy track into the village street, to pass the church on your left and a telephone box on your right.

Walk 27 – Rutland Water

MANTON • RUTLAND WATER • LYNDON • WING
A 5 mile circuit from the south shore of Rutland Water.

Please note that permission is needed to walk along one small mile stretch of track between Manton and Rutland Water. To receive this permission you need to write to The Anglian Water Authority Headquarters, Oundle, Rutland. The Water authority has never been known to refuse this permission, and it is a somewhat irritating procedure...but it may be easier than arguing with anyone who tries to dissuade you from using the route!

Manton is half way between Oakham and Uppingham. It is only 4 miles from Hambleton, and you could easily do this walk on the same day as you do the Hambleton one, if you move by car between the two walks. Ideally, spread these Rutland Water walks over two days. (You could perhaps spend a night at Oakham or Uppingham and enjoy two consecutive days walking.)

From Manton walk past the little church with its distinctive double bell tower and down Priory Road, at the foot of Stocks Hill. Follow Priory Road as it swings right, passing the church on your right. *At the end of this 'pudding bag' cul de sac, there are lovely views to your left over the lake. Lax Hill is the first little peninsula, with the Hambleton peninsula beyond. Beyond the far shore Burley Hall stands on the skyline.*

Go through the gate. The field has a ridged gulley running along the middle of it. Follow the gulley across the field, passing a little lake and a spring in a cutting on your left.

Go through the farm gate and keep the hedge on your right. This curves round left to a gate with a notice 'Permit holders only. Follow Edith Weston signs. All dogs must be on leads.' (This is where your permission is needed.) The farm track straight ahead of you is private but leads directly to Lyndon Information centre. The Nature reserve is slightly left of the

track, behind wire fencing. The next gate is locked, to keep Nature reserve visitors away from the farm track. There is a stile to the left of it. Swing left to reach Lyndon Information centre and then turn right for a few yards to meet the access road. Turn left at the road and note the gate straight ahead, where the road swings right. Our path (which is also a cycle track) goes straight ahead, but you may need to turn right and follow the road for a few yards to reach the start of the path, as the gate ahead of you is padlocked against traffic and the footpath is fenced off.

Continue along the reservoir track. After a quarter of a mile, at the bottom of the hill, just before the track bends to the right, there is a wooden cattle pen enclosure in the field on your right.

Go through the cattle pen and continue uphill with the fence on your left. At the fence corner you need to swing left to continue diagonally uphill across the open field. There is a small wood at the top of the hill and you need to make for the far left corner of it.

At the end of the wood you need to turn right to walk up a little tussocky bit of the field, towards a barn. Go through the gate in the fence below the barn and go slightly left uphill to reach a bridle gate in the short stretch of top hedge. Now follow the hedge on your right and go to the main road ahead of you. Turn left and walk along the road for 200 yards until you are level with Edith Weston farm over to your left. On your right there is an opening which leads into a straight green track between hedges. (Ignore the small offshoot of path to your right.)

The green track, which may be a bit overgrown, leads you onto a wide cutting which goes straight through Lyndon Wood. This is lovely ancient mixed woodland and the path is usually easy to follow. (Look for the huge hollow oak!) It ends by descending to a dip beyond which is a farm gate.

In the open field move uphill to your left, to meet the road on your right at a gate and a footpath sign. Turn left and walk along the road through the beautiful stone village of Lyndon, past the lovely hall and church on your right.

St Martin's church at Lyndon, with its lovely graveyard, is worth a stop. A welcoming notice invites you to picnic, but please help to keep it tidy and preserve the flowers.

The road continues past a telephone box and a cross roads, with North Luffenham Road to your left. You need to continue straight ahead, along the road signposted to Wing.

After 100 yards turn right at the footpath sign.

From Lyndon to Wing, you are now going to walk on a path which has recently been diverted from its original straight line across the fields. The landowner was granted permission to move the path right round the edges of his fields, provided that a good unploughed headland path be left. This circuitous route is difficult to describe and not easy to follow. It is not yet waymarked and the good headland is often skimpy and in places non existent.

Go past the ha ha wall of Lyndon

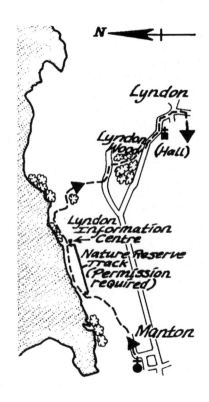

rectory to your right and continue following the hedge on your right as it bends round the edge of the field, passing the bottom of gardens.

Pass the elegant little cupula tower of Lyndon Hall and continue past the ha ha wall. At the end of the field turn left and walk with a belt of trees on your right.

When the woodland on your right begins to swing left you will be level with a tall isolated tree in the field on your left. Here you need to turn right to cross through the belt of trees.

Go downhill through a bridle gate and up the bank on the far side of the belt of trees.

You now need to walk close to the hedge which is now on your left. (Move left to reach it.) Follow this hedge, keeping in a westerly direction and walk the whole length of this huge field. (It was once two huge fields and you need to move left and then right at the old field junction to keep walking with the hedge on your left.)

You will be walking parallel with the railway line in the valley on your left. Eventually you will reach a plantation of willow and alder trees on your left near the corner of the field.

Cross the stile and footbridge in the corner of the field and turn left along the field road. Walk uphill with the hedge on your left. Cross the level crossing (Stop, Look and Listen!) and continue up the hill to meet the road.

You need to turn right to go into Wing, but if you haven't visited Wing Maze, this is your chance! It lies 200 yards up the road opposite you. It's not very spectacular but is of interest as a medieval penance maze, where penitents possibly traced the path on their knees, with suitable prayers until they reached the centre.

Walk through Wing village, passing the two pubs (The Cuckoo and The King's Arms) on your left and the general stores on your right. Turn right, down Middle Street which is almost opposite The King's Arms, and left along Bottom Street.

At the end of Bottom Street, just before it bends left to become Reeves Road, there is a footpath sign on your right.

Go through the gate by the sign and walk diagonally left downhill

towards the stream and the railway. *Note the way ahead. You are making for a junction of two railway lines. The old goods yard lies in front of you. To the left of it is a brick structure surmounting the brick arch of the railway bridge. The power lines lead directly to this point. The bridge is your next goal.*

To reach the railway bridge you need to cross the hedge on your left between two big ash trees. Move across the corner of the next field down towards the stream where you will find a substantial footbridge to cross.

Swing left and walk across this little field parallel with the railway line on your right. Cross the hedge in front of you at a ricketty gate and walk towards the railway bridge. Walk under the bridge and turn right to leave the road and walk between the brick engine shed and the railway line, along a little fenced off path which rises gradually past the goods yard on your right.

Pass to the right of a house with stables, passing on your left a brick igloo, a railway ventilation shaft, where the railway goes through a tunnel and under the village of Manton. A kissing gate on your right takes you up a little fenced off path beside the house drive.

Emerge on the wide lane between houses (Southview Close). Turn left along the main road and then right, along Stocks Hill, to reach Manton church, where you started the walk.

Is the pub open for a drink? or are you going to one of the many cafes or restaurants in Oakham? Either would round off a perfect day!

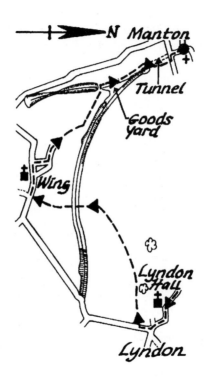

There are so many interesting books on Leicesteshire and Rutland that it is impossible to mention them all. The ones to which I am most indebted are:

W.G.Hoskins: *The Heritage of Leicestershire 1972*
    The Making of the English Landscape 1955
    Rutland (Leicester City Publication)1949
    Rutland: A Shell Guide. Faber 1963
    Touring Leicesteshire 1948-71
Nikolaus Pevsner: *The Buildings of England:* Penguin 1960
Arthur Mee: *The King's England:* (Hodder and Stoughton 1937)
Ekwall, E. *The Concise Oxford Dictionary of English Place Names.* 1936.
Nicholls: *Antiquities 1798-1800*
Guy Paget and Lionel Irvine: *Leicestershire 1950*
J.B.Firth: *Highways and Byways in Leicestershire* 1926
Victoria County History 1908-35 1964
Rev J.H.Hill *History of the Parish of Langton* 1867
Celia Fiennes *The Journey of Celia Fiennes*
Hugh Collinson: *Rural Rides in Historic Leicestershire* 1981
Jonathan Wilshire: *The Rev.William Hanbury 1725-1778 of Church Langton*
J.D.Bennett: *Discovering Leicestershire* 1970